S0-AWR-693

Illustrators 21

THE TWENTY FIRST ANNUAL EXHIBITION OF ILLUSTRATION HELD IN THE GALLERIES OF THE
SOCIETY OF ILLUSTRATORS, 128 EAST 63RD STREET, NEW YORK, FEBRUARY 7 THROUGH APRIL 11, 1979

Copyright © 1980 by Society of Illustrators, Inc.
All rights reserved
No part of this book may be reproduced, stored in a retrieval system, or transmitted
in any form or by any means, electronic, mechanical, photocopying, recording or otherwise,
without the prior permission of the publishers.
ISBN 8038-3427-6
Library of Congress Catalog Card Number 59-10849
Printed in the United States of America

Distributors
CANADA: Saunders of Toronto, Ltd., Don Mills, Ontario
BENELUX, SCANDINAVIA & ITALY: Graphic Art and Design, Futura-Verlag, Lindenstrasse 35,
    8008 Zurich, Switzerland
FRANCE: Graphis Distribution, Milon-La-Chapelle, F-78470 St-Remy-Les Chevreuse
SPAIN: Liberia Cientifica, Preciados 38, E-Madrid 13
SWITZERLAND: Arthur Niggli, Ltd., Publishers, CH-9052 Niederteufen
All other countries: Fleetbooks, S.A., c/o Feffer and Simons, Inc., 100 Park Avenue, New York 10017

GERALD McCONNELL *Editor*   ROBERT HALLOCK *Designer*

Illustrators 21

THE TWENTY FIRST ANNUAL OF AMERICAN ILLUSTRATION

Published for the Society of Illustrators by **HASTINGS HOUSE, PUBLISHERS, INC.,** New York 10016

We would like to thank and properly credit the following who served on the jury for the Society's previous Annual Exhibition, ILLUSTRATORS 20, but were inadvertently omitted from that edition of the Annual Book.

ILLUSTRATORS 20 JURORS

ADVERTISING
Shannon Stirnweis, *Chairman*
Jerry Alten
Walter Bernard
Bernie D'Andrea
Elaine Duillo
Roger Huyssen
Alvin J. Pimsler
Cal Sacks

EDITORIAL
Chuck McVicker, *Chairman*
Carol Carson
Bill Charmatz
Bob Grossman
Mike Hooks
Sandy Kossin
Randy Ross
Rolf Siljander
Teresa Woodward

BOOK
Bob Peak, *Chairman*
Guy Billout
Bart Forbes
Mariah Graham
Bob Handville
Wilson McLean
Gordon Mortensen
Saul Tepper

INSTITUTIONAL
Isadore Seltzer, *Chairman*
Tom Allen
Walter Aravelo
John Berg
Roland Descombes
Jim McMullan
Howard Paine
Warren Rogers
Daniel Schwartz

TV/FILM
Barney Plotkin, *Chairman*
Tom Daly
Barbara Effron
Robert J. Lee
Neil Shakery
Charles B. Slackman

Illustrators 21

THE SOCIETY OF ILLUSTRATORS

OFFICERS

Honorary President	Harold Von Schmidt
President	Warren Rogers
Executive Vice President	John Witt
Vice President	Arthur Weithas
Treasurer	Walter Hortens
Associate Treasurer	Diane Dillon
Secretary	Murray Tinkelman
House Chairman	Gerald McConnell

ILLUSTRATORS 21 COMMITTEE

Chairwoman	Eileen Schultz
Associate Chairman	Sandy Huffaker
Annual Book Editor	Gerald McConnell
Annual Book Designer	Robert Hallock
Poster Designer	Eileen Schultz
Poster Artist	Robert Peak
Hanging Chairman	Arthur Weithas

STAFF

Executive Director	Arpi Ermoyan
Show Coordinator	Terry Brown
Show Staff	Jill Bossert
	Cathy Citarella
	Anna Lee Fuchs
	Norma Pimsler

ILLUSTRATORS 21 JURORS

ADVERTISING
Simms Taback, *Chairman*
Marshall Arisman
Robert Bach
David Blossom
Dick Gangel
Ellen Griesdieck
Irene Ramp
Boris Vallejo
Art Weithas

EDITORIAL
Howard Koslow, *Chairman*
Ray Ameijide
Grace Clarke
Bob Cunningham
Marion Davis
David Grove
Eugene Light
Fred Otnes

BOOK
Harry Schaare, *Chairman*
John DeCesare
Lou Dorfsman
Linda Fennimore
George Tscherny
Don Weller
Noel Werrett
Reagan Wilson

INSTITUTIONAL
Roger Huyssen, *Chairman*
John Collier
Everett Davidson
Madlyn Dickens
Bernie Fuchs
H. Tom Hall
Janet McCaffrey
James Plumeri
Carol Wald

TV/FILM
Jacqui Morgan, *Chairman*
Sandy Huffaker
Doug Johnson
Jerry McConnell

ILLUSTRATORS 21 by Warren Rogers, President 1978-1980

ILLUSTRATORS 21, the first of our third decade of annuals! Quite obviously, these 21 books are the finest record anywhere of American illustration (and in recent years, world-wide illustration).

It's hard to imagine how any group of jurors can distill more than 5,000 pieces of art down to the 500 or so that appear in this book. 45 people did it and their choices are superb. New techniques by old friends. Fresh new work by artists unknown to the Society. Every show brings new surprises and excitement over young artists entering our world. And this year's annual bears this out.

The Society is very grateful to those people who worked so hard to make "21" happen: Chairwoman Eileen Schultz, the juries, the staff, the crew who hung the show and all the artists from around the world who, after all, are its heroes.

ILLUSTRATORS 21 by Eileen Schultz, Show Chairman

Each year the statement heard most frequently before an SI Annual Exhibition is that it will be impossible to surpass the great work done the previous year, and then the show opens and again it's a truly magnificent collection of talent.

This year was no exception and as Chairwoman I can attest to the difficulty the committees had in making their final selections out of approximately 5,000 fine national and international entries received.

As for the planning and follow-through that brings about a successful show, grateful thanks go to the distinguished judges who gave of their valuable time and expert talent; to the gallery committee whose time, planning and effort should not be overlooked; and most of all to Arpi and her superb staff at the Society, who continually perform with such admirable efficiency and good spirit.

I know you will enjoy this volume of ILLUSTRATORS 21 and continued success to all and to our profession.

EDITOR'S STATEMENT by Gerald McConnell

As Publishing Coordinator for the Society and Editor of this year's Annual Book, I would like to take this opportunity to thank everyone who has helped bring this volume to fruition. Special cudos to Terry Brown for his articles on our Hall of Famers, to Jill Bossert for her Hamilton King Award article, to Gerry Gersten for his memorable caricatures in the front section, to Bob Hallock for once again designing a very classy Annual and, of course, to Russell Neale and Jim Moore at Hastings House for their tireless efforts on our behalf.

DESIGNERS'S COMMENT by Robert Hallock

Gerry Gersten's caricatures probably reveal our true personalities in contrast to Bernie Fuchs' gracious portraits in last year's Annual. Gersten has captured the accurate image of me upon completing involvement with still another book. I should know after four of them!

ILLUSTRATORS 21 is an intriguing compilation of the year's work. The great variety of expression shows the vitality of American illustration today. The additional International Section reflects its influence abroad. It is indeed an indispensible source book documenting our times for a permanent record. I trust that it will inspire ever new dimensions in the years ahead.

HALL OF FAME—
EDWIN AUSTIN ABBEY (1852-1911)

Edwin Austin Abbey was that rare union of "fun and purpose." He was cherished by the many organizations which called him "fellow." Those who called him "friend" included the most renowned artists, sculptors and authors of his day. But his artwork was his purpose. He illustrated with crisp pen lines, painted with shadowy, mysterious tones and he designed decorative and architecturally sound murals. Every endeavor of his career was totally absorbing of his energy but was executed with grace and humor. Howard Pyle described his contemporary as a "chipper, jocund little fellow, with a merry twinkle of his eyes and a laugh that meant business."

"Ned" Abbey was born in Philadelphia on April 1, 1852. His poor but cultured parents encouraged his artistic talents as he apprenticed to landscape artist Isaac Williams and engravers Van Ingen and Snyder. At the Pennsylvania Academy of the Fine Arts (1868-1871) he studied what he called "the science of constructive drawing." Throughout his career he was a believer in drawing from life and spent hours at his sketchbooks. He wrote to a young art student: "You should be sketching always. Draw the dishes on the table while you are waiting for breakfast. Draw the people on the station while you are waiting for the train. It is all part of your world. You are going to be one of a profession to which everything on earth means something."

He had been submitting drawings to Harper & Brothers for two years before the first was published (12/3/1870). Charles Parsons, Art Editor, had established *Harper's Weekly* and *The Monthly Magazine* as America's top illustrated journals. In 1871, Abbey joined their staff in New York which included Charles Reinhart, the Waud brothers and others who quickly became his close friends. Will Low, his boyhood pen pal, soon joined the staff.

From 1871-1874, Abbey concentrated on English scenes for Herrick's poems and works by Shakespeare. These pen and ink drawings echoed Abbey's faithfulness to detail and drawing from life (even if it was a fellow staff artist who modeled). He moved into Winslow Homer's former studio on Washington Square and freelanced his work to *Harper's*. Many lucrative offers came his way but he remained faithful to the man who gave him "an opportunity," Charles Parsons.

In 1878, two years after the Centennial Exposition in Philadelphia which included many English works which Abbey termed "eyeopeners," *Harper's* sponsored his move to England. He settled in the Cotswold region by the Avon River. He soon befriended many of England's top talents. George Boughton, Frank Millet and Alfred Parsons are but a few who traveled and sketched with Abbey throughout Europe. "Sketching Rambles in Holland" was the product of one such trip.

During the 1880's, *Harper's* was bursting with Abbey drawings for Herrick's poems, Goldsmith's "She Stoops to Conquer," and two collections of anecdotes and songs illustrated by Abbey ("Old Songs" and "The Quiet Life"). These projects were time-consuming and with Abbey's penchant for costumes, models and settings his income suffered.

Harper's, minus the now retired Parsons, launched their Comedies of Shakespeare series in 1889 and Abbey received the commission. He began to paint in oils and those who viewed the Royal Academy's Exhibition for 1890 saw his first exhibited oil. There was instant acclaim. In August of that year he married Mary Gertrude Mead, a well-educated New York socialite and they returned to England. Abbey wrote of her in 1910: "A painter's finished work is given to the world, and the public generally may see it, but very few can know whence his greatest inspirations and his highest aspirations have been drawn. In saying this I am doing scant justice to one who has been my daily and hourly companion and counselor and friend these twenty years."

Their home in Gloucestershire, Morgan Hall, became a summer spa for such notables as Charles Dana Gibson, Augustus St. Gaudens, Stanford White, Henry James, James McNeill Whistler, Mark Twain and Arthur Conan Doyle. Music, The Artists Cricket Club and sketching parties were their favorite pastimes. Abbey's London studio, Chelsea Lodge, was also a popular spot and was frequently used by his close friend, John Singer Sargent.

During the 1890's, Abbey was busy on several commissions, the most extensive being the murals for the Boston Public Library. In 1895, the first finished work "King Arthur and the Holy Grail," was exhibited to overflow crowds in New York. He was acclaimed a superior muralist. Scribner's obtained the reproduction rights and many of Abbey's debts were settled. As Mrs. Abbey put it, "We're now penniless and free."

In the summer of 1901, The Tragedies of Shakespeare were commissioned and they appeared in *Harper's* through 1909. This decade also saw his painting of the coronation of Queen Victoria's successor, Edward VII, at the new King's request. This was a major honor for an American artist.

While on holiday in Pennsylvania in 1902, Abbey visited the architect for the new Capitol buildings in Harrisburg. He came away with his last and most ambitious mural assignment. The decorations for this complex included several murals and lunettes. Abbey completed the large Capitol mural before he died and the sketches for the unfinished sections were faithfully completed by John Singer Sargent and others at Mrs. Abbey's request.

The ever-strong and energetic Ned spent but a few weeks in sick bed before he died in England of a liver ailment on August 1, 1911. He was 59.

—*Terry Brown*

HALL OF FAME—LORRAINE FOX
(1922-1976)

An artist's world is a special place where emotions co-exist with the realities of life. When this world emerges on paper or canvas through the artist's talented hand, we outsiders are given an "audience" with these emotions and a glimpse into this world.

Lorraine Fox's world was unique. The images and symbolism, the brushwork and experimental media were uniquely hers. Nostalgic but youthful, disciplined but everchanging, she was an inspiration to her closest friends, to her students and to all those who "swim upstream." For she was determined early in her life to make it in this profession at a time when women were the exception.

Born in Brooklyn of second generation German and Irish parents, Lorraine had a youthful talent for art. Her brother, a cartoonist, brought humor into her early life and her Victorian grandmother gave her a fondness for nostalgia. These traits are seen in her earliest published works but there would be stronger influences down the road.

She graduated from Pratt Institute in 1944 and obtained a staff position at Keiswetter Agency. Limited to spots at this time, she also freelanced work to *Seventeen* and *Better Homes and Gardens*. Kirk Wilkenson, art director at *Woman's Day*, was the first to see the full potential in this determined young woman. Her regular column of drawings as well as full illustrations appeared in that magazine. One fact rings true. Even in the simplest and smallest assignment Lorraine added touches of her own creativity and imagination.

One of Lorraine's sharpest competitors at Pratt had been Bernard D'Andrea. After graduation he became her ardent suitor and in 1951 they were married in New York City. His reputation as an illustrator was being established in *The Saturday Evening Post*, *Ladies Home Journal* and *Good Housekeeping* in the heyday of the boy-girl era. They were a positive influence on each other's artwork as their styles grew closer.

In the mid 1950's Lorraine joined Bernie at the Charles E. Cooper Studio. This amalgam of artists was the center for illustration talent at that time. Joe DeMers, Steve Dohanos, Alex Ross, Jon Whitcomb and Coby Whitmore were in Cooper's stable. Lorraine developed in this atmosphere but a strong influence lay ahead.

In 1961, she enrolled in Ruben Tam's painting class at the Brooklyn Museum Art School. His theories on introspection and emotional expression were to bring her subconscious to the fore. Her paintings took on a more profound reality, losing much of their naïvité. Her four years of study with Tam were to develop her as an illustrator but her personal works, though unseen even today, would please any gallery.

The D'Andreas worked very closely though in separate studios of their Great Neck, N.Y. home. Annual travels, most often to Europe, were times for sketching and for shopping for the many art items which decorated their home.

The long working relationship which Lorraine had with the publications in the women's magazine market attests to the respect with which her works were held. *Redbook*, *Cosmopolitan* and *Good Housekeeping* were clients of hers for many years. Her untimely death came at a point in her development when she was painting some of her best works and was nearing the elusive goal called "satisfaction."

Lorraine's influence on illustration, however, will be felt for many years to come through her active role in the shaping of young artists at Parsons School of Design and at the Famous Artists School. Many of Ruben Tam's theories found their way into her classroom. She inspired her students to find themselves through their work and to feel the exhilaration of that self discovery.

—*Terry Brown*

HALL OF FAME—
BENJAMIN ALBERT STAHL (b. 1910)

With a thirsty curiosity, a young Ben Stahl and his paternal grandmother would linger for hours in the Chicago Art Institute and other local galleries. His parents, both of German ancestry, encouraged his interest in literature and art as he devoured Horatio Alger and Tarzan. When his interest in the required public schooling dwindled, the Art Institute granted him an opportunity to learn from their masters. He was soon exhibiting in their shows.

Stahl found time to practice between errand chores at Young, Timmins and Smith Studios but as the depression grew darker in the early 1930's he had to settle for "unpaid" status. In 1932, with determination and talent, he approached the offices of Stevens, Sundblom and Stults, Chicago's top studio with such known, and soon to be known, talents on hand as Haddon Sundblom, Matt Clark, Ward Brackett and Coby Whitmore. Stahl's portfolio made his case. He remained with Stevens until 1937 with only a short stint at the Chicago *Daily News*. Stahl said: "I would advise every young student of art to spend some time on a newspaper, preferably early in his career. But don't stay too long. Get a certain amount of experience, which will be invaluable later —then get out."

He worked for several studios in Chicago and Detroit as his exposure as an illustrator grew. After he had painted a series of advertisements for Cutler-Hammer, he was contacted by *The Saturday Evening Post*. His star was gathering speed. During his first four years with *The Post* he was typed as an illustrator of sea stories even though the midwesterner had never seen a body of water larger than the Great Lakes. His illustrations for C. S. Forester's "Captain Horatio Hornblower" are among his best works of this era. An award-winning advertising series for Bell Aircraft added greater luster to his star. Stahl's freelance career loomed ahead.

In late 1940, he married Ella Lehocky. They moved to New York City in 1943 and the following year to Westport, Connecticut. Their home and nearby studio were ideal for the creative artist and his growing family. Ben took an active membership in the Westport Artists and the Society of Illustrators.

The Saturday Evening Post remained his bread-and-butter editorial client. Frank Kilker, its editor in the 1940's, held the most intriguing manuscripts for Stahl to illustrate. Also on his editorial list were the *American* Magazine, *Coronet, Woman's Home Companion* and *Esquire*.

The National Academy of Design bestowed its highest award, the Saltus Gold Medal, on Stahl for his painting "Circus People" which he completed shortly after a trip to the Ringling Circus headquarters in Sarasota, Florida in 1949. The family moved to Siesta Key, near there, in the early 1950's.

One of Stahl's most ambitious projects began in 1954 when he was commissioned by the Catholic Press to paint "the finest Stations of the Cross ever conceived by artistic or spiritual standards." Extensive research in Jerusalem followed and in 1958 the paintings and drawings were exhibited at the Society of Illustrators. In the mid-1960's The Museum of the Cross was being established in Sarasota. Stahl designed the building and painted 15 large murals of the "Way of the Cross." The Museum was vandalized shortly after its completion and these works were never recovered.

His entry into the children's fiction market was an immediate success. "Blackbeard's Ghost" (Houghton Mifflin, 1965) was a Sequoia National Award winner from the Oklahoma Library Association. "The Secret of Red Skull," "Happy Exile" and "Cry Rosa Cry Death" followed.

Ben Stahl's theories on art have found many forums. From the earliest days as a student instructor at the Chicago Art Institute to the founding of the Famous Artists School, from the series of lectures, "Journey into Art," for Educational Television to his present home in San Miguel Allende, near Mexico City, he has emphasized the need for drawing, observation and careful composition.

As one of America's most versatile talents, he has been recognized for excellence in many fields. As an illustrator he will always be known for a more open form of expression, more precise composition and more free-flowing drama in his work. He makes the eye, and the heart, move on the canvas. Art Directors who saved their most challenging and most difficult tasks for Ben Stahl were never disappointed.

—Terry Brown

HAMILTON KING AWARD—
WILLIAM TEASON (b.1922)

Bill Teason comes on soft-spoken and sweet— a gentle man. But as one looks through a stack of samples and hears his soothing voice describe them, one is shocked by the blood, gore and mystery displayed: the startled, staring corpse of an old woman in a bathtub, children with the devil in their eyes and an endless procession of dripping daggers, scattered jewels and false eyeballs. These are the result of Mr. Teason's long and steady career as a mystery paperback book artist.

Mr. Teason was born in Kansas City, Missouri in 1922. His father was a printer who brought home newsprint, pencils and encouragement to Bill and his two brothers. Drawing became Bill's only interest and it was nurtured by his High School teacher, Mabel Newitt, who was instrumental in getting him a scholarship to the Kansas City Art Institute. He took his good fortune lightly and left after six months. After four years in the Air Force Bill came to New York. He went to the famous Cooper Studio where he was *not* hired, but where Mr. Cooper told him Winsor & Newton Designer Colors were best. Bill uses them to this day. He *did* get a job at Sudler and Hennessey where Herb Lubalin helped him catch up on much that he had missed in school.

From 1947 to 1951 he worked on the *Lederle Bulletin* doing a monthly series called "Art Treasures from the Metropolitan Museum of Art." The subjects were a pleasure to work on and served as a polishing stone for his technique. Disenchanted with much of his advertising work, Bill went freelance in 1951. It was Walter Brooks at Dell who got him started on the career that still keeps him very busy. In 1957 he did the first of over 200 Agatha Christie mystery covers, covers which feature clues—sinister still lifes. In addition to Dell, Popular Library and Fawcett are regular clients. Teason's mysterious touch has crossed over into the movie poster field. His "*Night Visitor,*" done for Bill Gold Advertising, won a Los Angeles Art Directors Club Award. He's also the recipient of the Mystery Writers' Raven Award for the cover of "*Picture Miss Seeton.*"

As a boy Bill was fond of rainy nights and lightning bolts, Sherlock Holmes and Charlie Chan. His feeling that life is a mystery remains. "What you see with your eyes is not really what is." That we are all unseen skeletons clanking around is an idea that fascinates him. His jugglers, bird-headed folks or melting wax people appear from "out of a fog." With only a small, sketchy preliminary drawing for reference, he starts with his multi-colored, muted backgrounds and then lays the figures down. Even if the subject is a child there is the feeling that forces unknown are at work outside our direct senses.

Whatever these forces are, people have been responding to them for over 20 years. Mr. Teason has shown his work at the Society, the National Academy and the American Watercolor Society where he has received numerous awards.

The Society is pleased to have chosen Bill Teason as our Hamilton King Award Winner, an artist who "is still an innocent" and still amazed at the mystery of our existence.

—*Jill Bossert*

THE TWENTY FIRST ANNUAL OF AMERICAN ILLUSTRATION

1
Editorial
Artist: **Frank Gallo**
Art Director: Arthur Paul/Kerig Pope
Publication: Playboy Magazine
Award for Excellence

2
Institutional
Artist: **Alan E. Cober**
Art Director: Alan E. Cober
Client: The Illustrators Workshop

3
Advertising
Artist: **Alan E. Cober**
Art Director: Alan E. Cober

4
Advertising
Artist: **Robert Weaver**
Art Director: Susan Eckrote/Richard Wilde
Client: School of Visual Arts
Gold Medal

NUESTRO

THE MAGAZINE FOR LATINOS

JULY, 1978 $1.25

PRESENTING

For Your

SUMMER READING PLEASURE

★ ★ ★

LATINO ★ TALENT ★ LATINO

★

Manolo the Martian Dwarf

In the Center Ring

and

A HORRIFYING TALE OF HUMILIATION!

✳

VIRGILIO THE AMAZING PINBALL WIZARD!

✳

LOVE AND DEATH ON THE BORDER'S TIGHTROPE!

PLUS. MORE

0   71486 02039   07

5
Editorial
Artist: **Salvador Bru**
Art Director: Joan Gramate
Publication: Nuestro Magazine

6
Advertising
Artist: **John Collier**
Art Director: John Collier
Client: Milton Newborn
Gold Medal

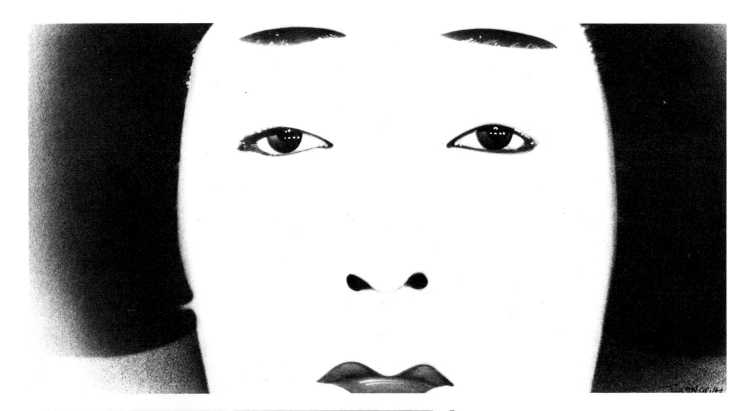

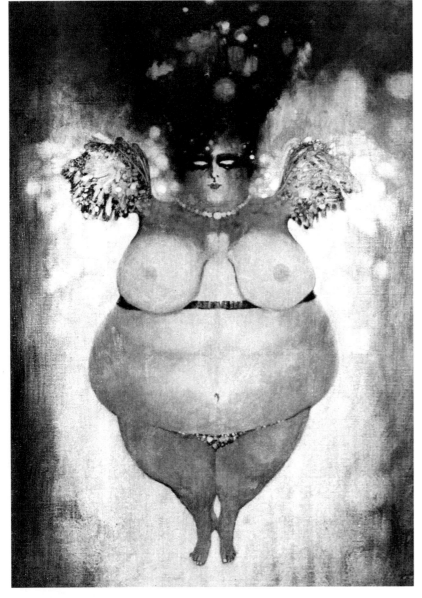

7
Institutional
Artist: **Steve Takenaga**
Art Director: Steve Takenaga
Client: J. Walter Thompson Co. — Detroit

8
Book
Artist: **Ted CoConis**
Art Director: Kristen Schleicher
Agency: Graphics International Design Group
Client: Graphics International Design Group

9
Editorial
Artist: **John Berkey**
Art Director: John Berkey
Award for Excellence

10
Advertising
Artist: **Ted CoConis**
Art Director: Kristen Schleicher
Agency: Graphics International Design Group
Client: Graphics International Design Group

11
Advertising
Artist: **Rick McCollum**
Art Director: Edgar Lansbury
Client: Lansbury-Beruh Productions

12
Advertising
Artist: **Robert Heindel**
Art Director: John deCesare
Agency: deCesare Design
Client: Geigy Pharmaceuticals

13
Book
Artist: **Carol Wald**
Art Director: Carol Wald

14
Editorial
Artist: **Jean-Paul Goude**
Art Director: Michael Brock
Publication: Oui Magazine

15
Book
Artist: **Eugene Karlin**
Art Director: E. A. Burke
Title: Psychology of Human Sexuality
Publisher: John Wiley & Sons, Inc.

16
Advertising
Artist: **Eugene Karlin**
Art Director: Joseph Nissen
Agency: Chalk, Nissen, Hanft, Inc.
Client: MEM Company, Inc.

17
Editorial
Artist: **Carol Wald**
Art Director: Maxine Davidowitz
Publication: Redbook Magazine

18
Institutional
Artist: **Michael Sell**
Art Director: Michael Sell

19
Book
Artist: **David Palladini**
Art Director: Skip Sorvino
Title: Real World English
Publisher: Scholastic Magazines, Inc.

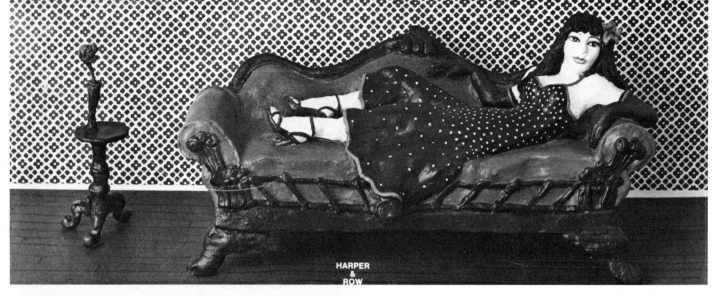

LA BELLE EDMÉE
A NOVEL BY SUZANNE PROU

LA BELLE EDMEE SUZANNE PROU

HARPER & ROW

20
Book
Artist: **Brookie Maxwell**
Art Director: Joan Kahn
Title: La Belle Edmee
Publisher: Harper & Row, Publishers, Inc.

21
Editorial
Artist: **Jacqui Morgan**
Art Director: Hans Baumeister
Publication: Novum Gebrauchs Graphik

22
Institutional
Artist: **Sue Llewellyn**
Art Director: Sue Llewellyn
Client: Jack Strong

23
Institutional
Artist: **Reagan Wilson**
Art Director: Tom Wood
Agency: Creative Services
Client: Collins, Miller & Hutchings

THE
EMPTY FACE
KATHARINA HAVEKAMP
A NOVEL

24
Book
Artist: **Gilbert Stone**
Art Director: Lynn Hollyn
Title: The Empty Face
Publisher: Richard Marek Publishers

25
Book
Artist: **David Passalacqua**
Art Director: Leonard Leone
Title: Looking on Darkness
Publisher: Bantam Books, Inc.

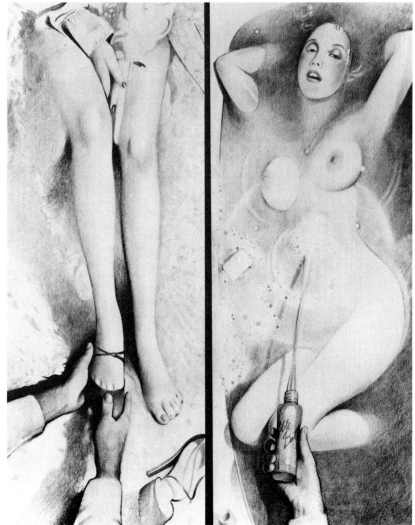

26
Editorial
Artist: **Martin Hoffman**
Art Director: Arthur Paul/T. Staebler
Publication: Playboy Magazine

27
Book
Artist: **Ron Villani**
Art Director: Ron Villani
Title: Yearbook of Science and the Future
Publisher: Encyclopaedia Britannica

28
Institutional
Artist: **Bob Peak**
Art Director: Eileen Hedy Schultz
Client: Society of Illustrators

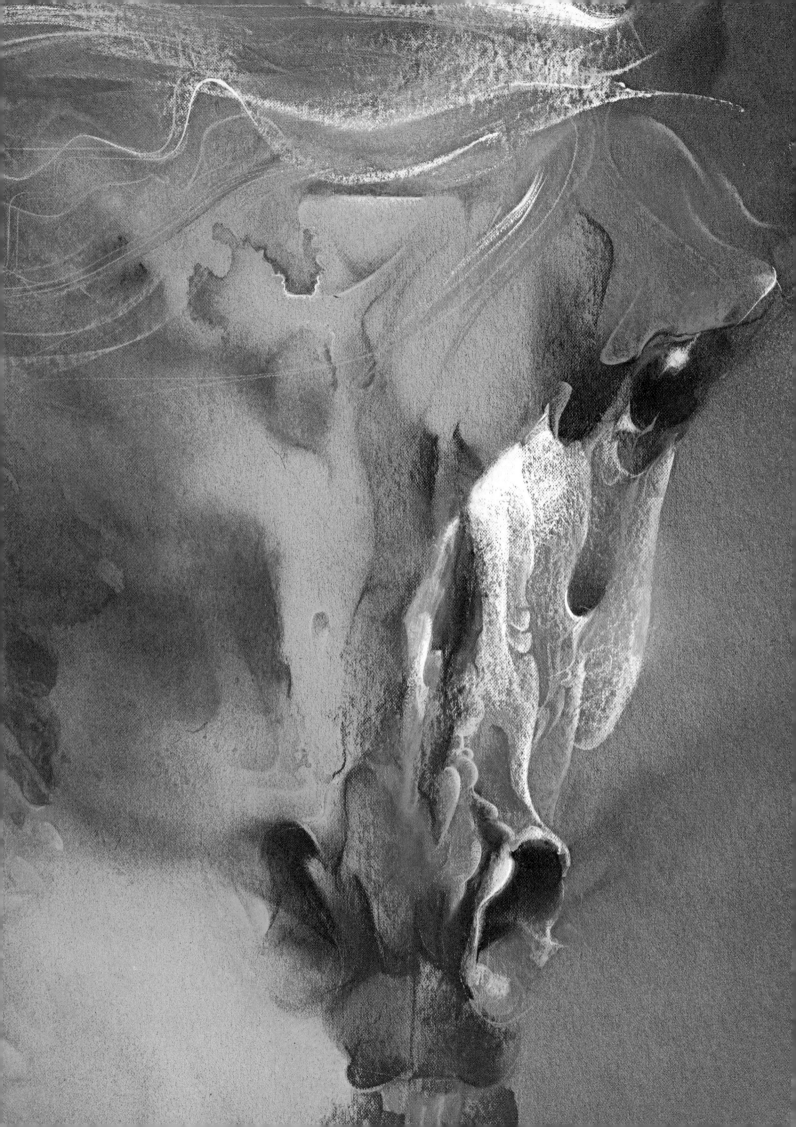

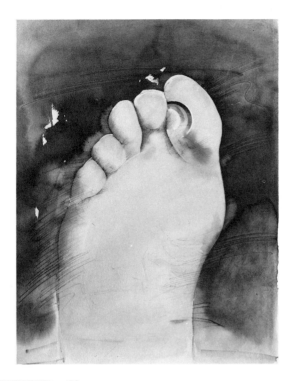

29
Institutional
Artist: **Paul Giovanopoulos**
Art Director: Paul Giovanopoulos

30
Editorial
Artist: **Robert Giusti**
Art Director: Joe Brooks
Publication: Penthouse Magazine

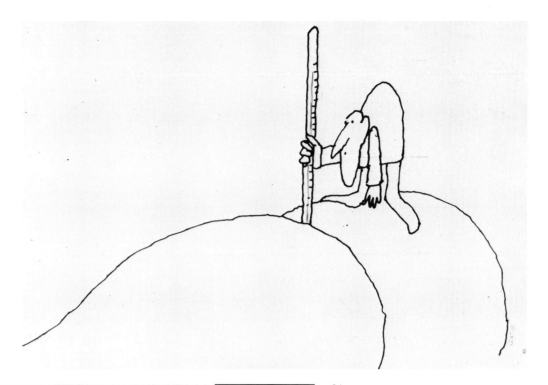

31
Book
Artist: **John T. Gatie**
Art Director: John T. Gatie

32
Book
Artist: **Richard Smith**
Art Director: Milton Charles
Title: My Secret Garden
Publisher: Pocket Books

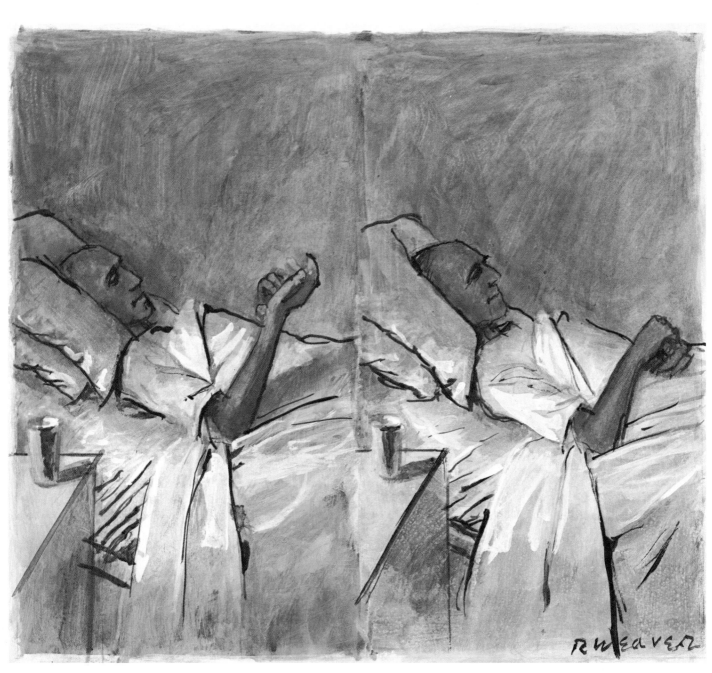

33
Advertising
Artist: **Robert Weaver**
Art Director: Alan J. Klawans
Client: Smith, Kline & French Laboratories

34
Book
Artist: **James Stevenson**
Art Director: Ava Weiss
Title: The Worst Person in the World
Publisher: Greenwillow Books

35
Advertising
Artist: **Reagan Wilson**
Art Director: Tom Wood
Client: Creative Services

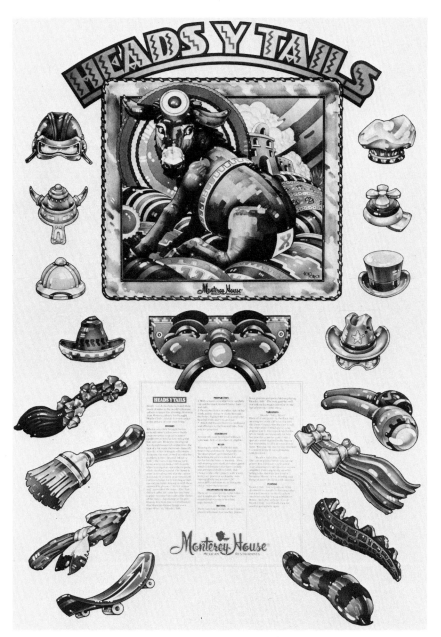

36
Advertising
Artist: **Doug Johnson**
Art Director: Chris Hill
Agency: Loucks Atelier
Client: Monterey House

37
Institutional
Artist: **Wendell Minor**
Art Director: Harris Lewine
Agency: Harris Lewine Produces
Client: Milton Newborn

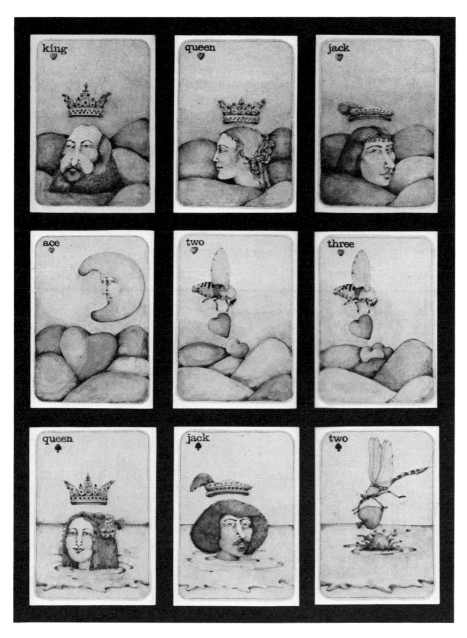

38
Institutional
Artist: **Dagmar Frinta**
Art Director: Dagmar Frinta

39
Book
Artist: **David Byrd**
Art Director: Barbara Bertoli
Title: Strong Poison
Publisher: Avon Books

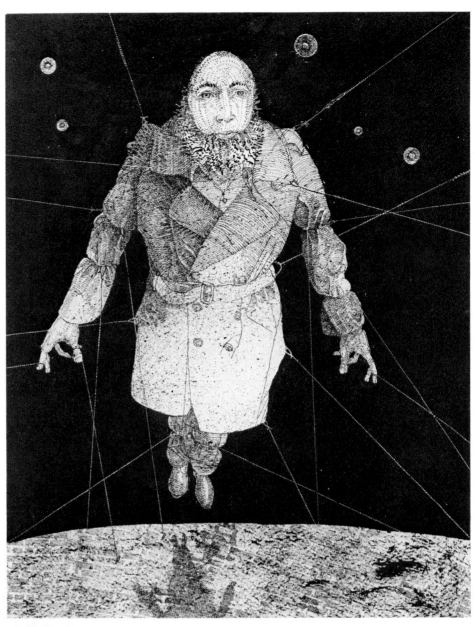

40
Editorial
Artist: **Alan E. Cober**
Art Director: Louise Kollembaum
Publication: Mother Jones Magazine

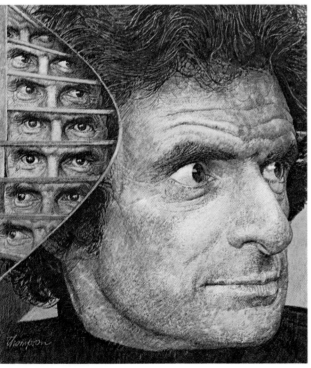

41
Book
Artist: **John Thompson**
Art Director: Leonard Leone
Title: Steps
Publisher: Bantam Books, Inc.

42
Editorial
Artist: **Richard Krepel**
Art Director: Tom Lennon
Publication: Emergency Medicine

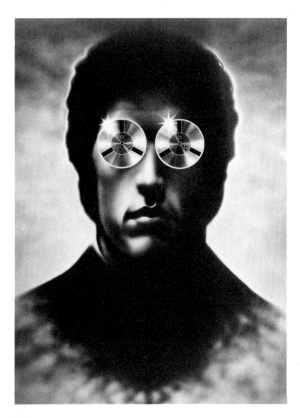

43
Book
Artist: **Paul Stinson**
Art Director: Frank Kozelek, Jr.
Title: The Oblivion Tapes
Publisher: Berkley Publishing Corp.

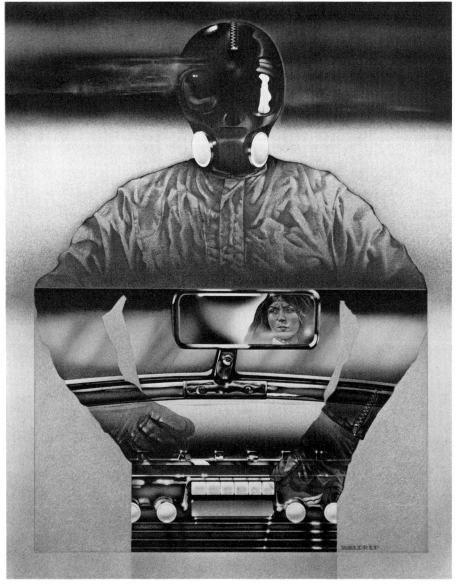

44
Editorial
Artist: **Richard L. Waldrep**
Art Director: Joe Brooks
Publication: Penthouse Magazine

45
Institutional
Artist: **Reagan Wilson**
Art Director: Mark English/Robert Heindel
Client: The Illustrators Workshop

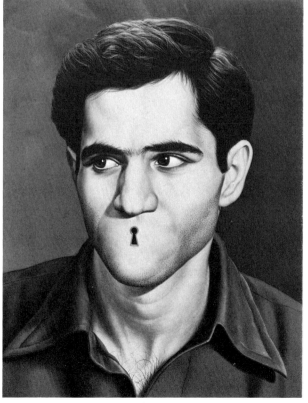

46
Editorial
Artist: **Eraldo Carugati**
Art Director: Arthur Paul/Kerig Pope
Publication: Playboy Magazine

47
Book
Artist: **Paul Vaccarello**
Art Director: Thomas Gorman
Title: The Land of the Dead
Publisher: Scott, Foresman & Co.

48
Book
Artist: **Walter Rane**
Art Director: Soren Noring
Title: Blood and Money
Publisher: Reader's Digest

49
Book
Artist: **Robert Heindel**
Art Director: William Gregory
Title: Psycho
Publisher: Reader's Digest

50
Book
Artist: **Richard Smith**
Art Director: Milton Charles
Title: In the Frame
Publisher: Pocket Books

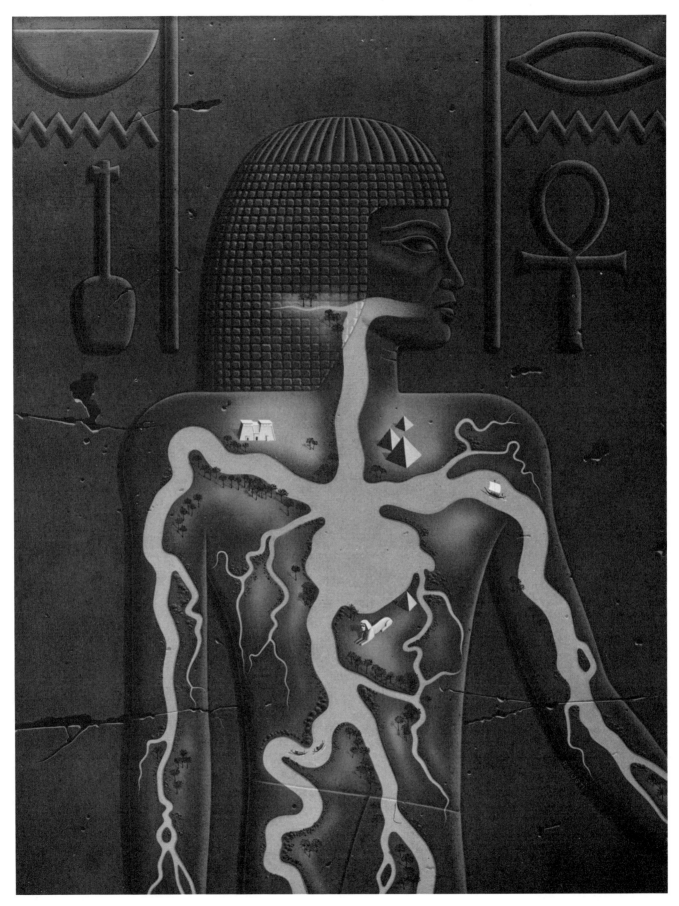

51
Institutional
Artist: **Robert Giusti**
Art Director: Peter Wong
Client: Ethyl Corp.
Award for Excellence

52
Advertising
Artist: **John Alcorn**
Art Director: Henrietta Condak
Client: CBS Records

53
Institutional
Artist: **Ben Chase**
Art Director: Ben Chase

November 2 1977
Crippled man was
spray painted by
3 youths. (corner
Broadway and 94th.
Marshall Arisman
Politicksmag - Urban Journal

54
Editorial
Artist: **Marshall Arisman**
Art Director: Mary Morgan
Publication: Politicks Magazine

55
Institutional
Artist: **Bob Ziering**
Art Director: Bob Ziering
Client: American Committee on Africa

56
Editorial
Artist: **Brad Holland**
Art Director: Pamela Vassil
Publication: The New York Times

57
Editorial
Artist: **Brad Holland**
Art Director: Cynthia Anderson
Publication: TriQuarterly

58
Editorial
Artist: **Brad Holland**
Art Director: Steve Heller
Publication: The New York Times Book Review

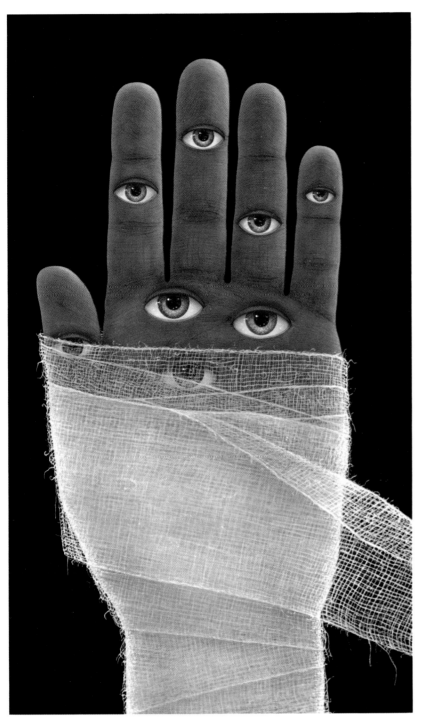

59
Book
Artist: **Don Brautigam**
Art Director: James Plumeri
Title: Night Shift
Publisher: New American Library

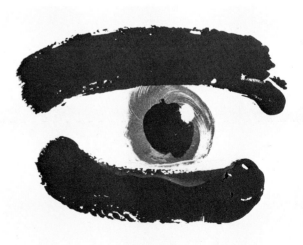

60
Institutional
Artist: **Carl Seltzer**
Art Director: Tom Ohmer
Agency: Advertising Designers, Inc.
Client: Pacific Health Resources, Inc.

61
Institutional
Artist: **Scott Greer**
Art Director: Micheal Richards
Agency: University Graphic Design
Client: Financial Aids
        University of Utah

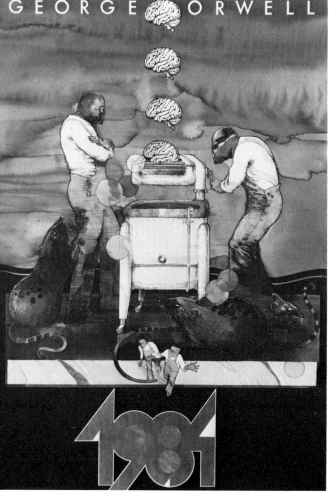

62
Book
Artist: **Mike Whitney**
Art Director: Mike Whitney

63
Book
Artist: **Diane Barr**
Art Director: Diane Barr

64
Institutional
Artist: **John Rush**
Art Director: John Rush
Client: Pema Browne Ltd.
Gold Medal

65
Editorial
Artist: **Richard Sparks**
Art Director: Carveth Kramer
Publication: Psychology Today

66
Editorial
Artist: **Peter Cox**
Art Director: Ron Campbell
Publication: Fortune Magazine

67
Editorial
Artist: **Jim Burns**
Art Director: John Workman
Publication: Heavy Metal Magazine

68
Editorial
Artist: **Gary Kelley**
Art Director: Dennis Knittig
Publication: TWA Ambassador

69
Advertising
Artist: **Bea Weidner**
Art Director: Bea Weidner

70
Editorial
Artist: **Chris Spollen**
Art Director: Chris Spollen
Publication: Quest/78

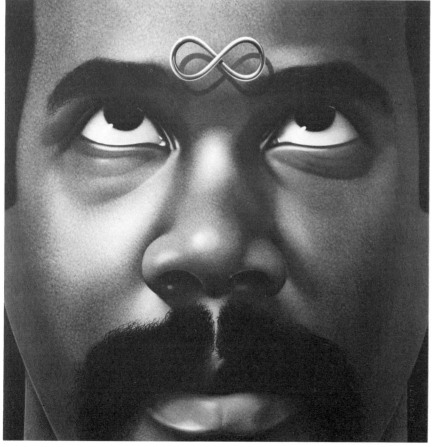

71
Advertising
Artist: **Robert Giusti**
Art Director: Lynn Dreese Breslin
Client: Atlantic Records

72
Advertising
Artist: **Phil Franké**
Art Director: Lawrence Danniels
Agency: Lawrence Danniels & Friends
Client: College Board

73
Advertising
Artist: **Eugene Mihaesco**
Art Director: John deCesare
Agency: deCesare Design
Client: Geigy Pharmaceuticals

74
Advertising
Artist: **Folon**
Art Director: Paula Scher
Client: CBS Records

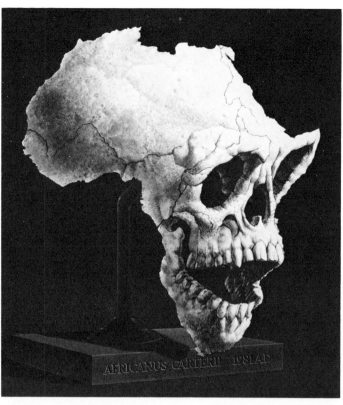

75
Editorial
Artist: **Don Ivan Punchatz**
Art Director: Joe Brooks
Publication: Penthouse Magazine

76
Editorial
Artist: **Alan Magee**
Art Director: Michael Brock/ Fred Nelson
Publication: Oui Magazine

77
Advertising
Artist: **Ed Scarisbrick**
Art Director: Tim Bryant
Agency: Gribbitt Design & Photography
Client: RCA Records

78
Editorial
Artist: **John Collier**
Art Director: Michael Brock
Publication: Oui Magazine

79
Institutional
Artist: **Carol Inouye**
Art Director: Carol Inouye
Client: Miranda Hine/Carol Inouye

80
Book
Artist: **Jözef Sumichrast**
Art Director: Harlin Quist
Title: Afraid Of The Dark
Publisher: Harlin Quist Books

81
Book
Artist: **Jözef Sumichrast**
Art Director: Harlin Quist
Title: Blackboard
Publisher: Harlin Quist Books

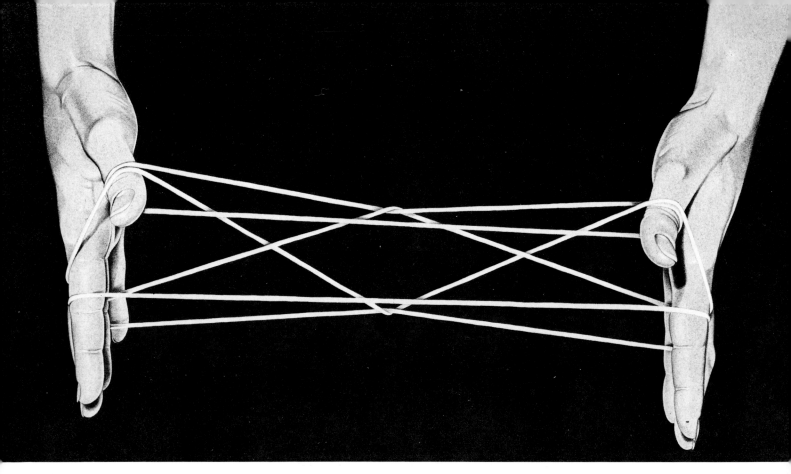

82
Book
Artist: **Sal Catalano**
Art Director: Skip Sorvino
Title: Relating to Others
Publisher: Scholastic Magazines

83
Book
Artist: **Ben F. Stahl**
Art Director: Margaret Frith
Title: Monsters of North America
Publisher: G.P. Putnam's Sons

84
Advertising
Artist: **Bob Ziering**
Art Director: Charles Schmalz
Agency: William Douglas McAdams
Client: Reed & Carnrick

85
Institutional
Artist: **Garry Colby**
Art Director: Gary Shortt
Client: McNamara Associates

86
Advertising
Artist: **Steve Tarantal**
Art Director: J. Robert Parker
Client: Smith, Kline & French Laboratories

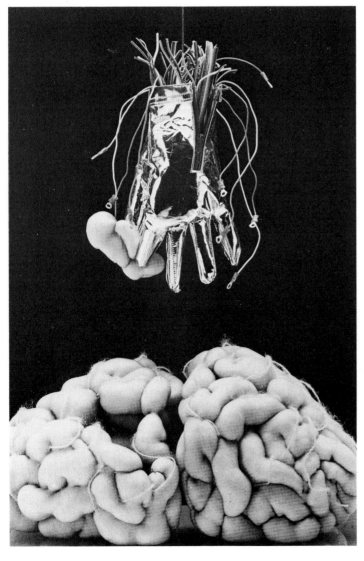

87
Editorial
Artist: **Carol Inouye**
Art Director: Carveth Kramer
Publication: Psychology Today

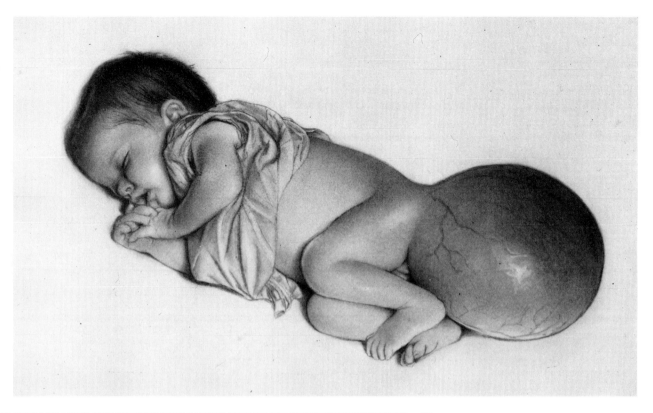

88
Institutional
Artist: **Sharon Ellis**
Art Director: Sharon Ellis

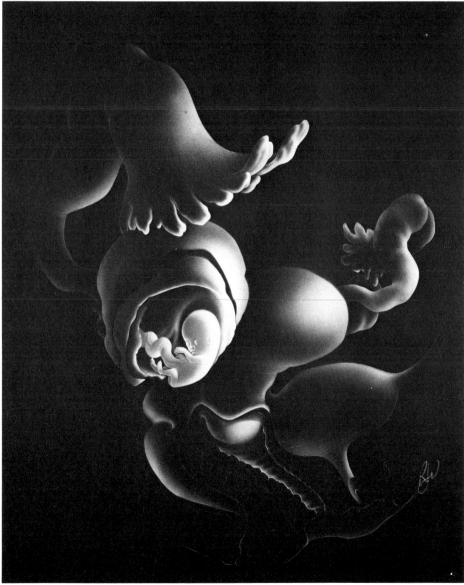

89
Institutional
Artist: **Robert J. Demarest**
Art Director: Robert J. Demarest
Client: College of Physicians & Surgeons

90
Book
Artist: **Bert Dodson**
Art Director: Lydia Halverson/Hal Kearney
Title: The Oyster and the Pearl
Publisher: Scott, Foresman & Company

91
Editorial
Artist: **Bernard Fuchs**
Art Director: Richard Gangel
Publication: Sports Illustrated

92
Editorial
Artist: **Alice Brickner**
Art Director: Ron Vareltzis
Publication: Creative Psychiatry 12

93
Institutional
Artist: **Mark McMahon**
Art Director: Mark McMahon

94
Institutional
Artist: **Jack Endewelt**
Art Director: Jack Endewelt

95
Book
Artist: **William Ersland**
Art Director: Neoma West
Title: Ideal Meal
Publisher: Meredith Publishing Co.

96
Book
Artist: **Kenneth Francis Dewey**
Art Director: Gordon Fisher
Publisher: The Franklin Library

97
Book
Artist: **Patric Fourshé**
Art Director: Patric Fourshé

98
Advertising
Artist: **Wilson McLean**
Art Director: Pat Chiono
Agency: Ogilvy & Mather Inc.
Client: Purpom Cider

99
Advertising
Artist: **Milton Glaser**
Art Director: Kevin Eggers
Client: The Tomato Music Co.

100
Institutional
Artist: **Isadore Seltzer**
Art Director: Mark Passy
Client: Copco, Inc.

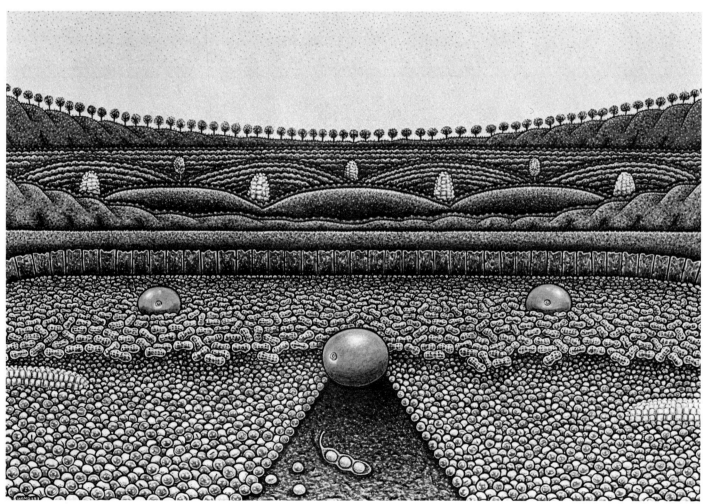

101
Book
Artist: **Steve Berman**
Art Director: Ron Villani
Title: Yearbook of Science and the Future
Publisher: Encyclopaedia Britannica

102
Book
Artist: **Al Tomba**
Art Director: Al Tomba

103
Advertising
Artist: **Richard Sparks**
Art Director: Paula Bisacca
Client: Nonesuch Records

104
Editorial
Artist: **Robert E. McGinnis**
Art Director: Salvatore Lazzarotti
Publication: Guideposts Magazine

105
Institutional
Artist: **Benjamin Eisenstat**
Art Director: Benjamin Eisenstat

106
Editorial
Artist: **William A. Motta**
Art Director: William A. Motta

107
Book
Artist: **Saul Mandel**
Art Director: Saul Mandel

108
Institutional
Artist: **Saul Mandel**
Art Director: Cam Hyers
Client: Hyers/Smith, Inc.

Nematodes (root knot and stunt). They make root ends swell up and rot. Slow growth. Stunt or kill young tobacco.

Wireworms. They chew off smaller roots. Burrow up into stem to damage tobacco.

109
Advertising
Artist: **Ray Ameijide**
Art Director: Roy Freemantle
Agency: Marsteller, Inc.
Client: Furadan

110
Book
Artist: **John Alcorn**
Art Director: Lynn Hollyn
Title: The Night of Trees
Publisher: Richard Marek Publishers

111
Editorial
Artist: **Yang Hsien-Min**
Art Director: Howard E. Paine
Publication: National Geographic

112
Book
Artist: **Richard Crist**
Art Director: Al Sherman
Title: Encyclopedia of Gardening
Publisher: Time/Life Books, Inc.

113
Editorial
Artist: **Tom O'Mary**
Art Director: Tom O'Mary

114
Book
Artist: **Wendell Minor**
Art Director: Lidia Ferrara
Title: River of Light
Publisher: Alfred A. Knopf, Inc.

115
Editorial
Artist: **Bradford Washburn**
Art Director: Howard E. Paine
Publication: National Geographic

116
Institutional
Artist: **Jack Unruh**
Art Director: Jack Summerford
Agency: Richards Group
Client: Triton

117
Institutional
Artist: **Reynold Ruffins**
Art Director: Reynold Ruffins
Agency: Reynold Ruffins, Inc.
Client: Children's Book Council

118
Advertising
Artist: **John Alcorn**
Art Director: Paula Scher
Client: CBS Records

119
Institutional
Artist: **John Alcorn**
Art Director: Lou Dorfsman/Ira Teichberg
Client: CBS Inc.

120
Book
Artist: **Gerry Gersten**
Art Director: Connie Timm
Title: Caribbean Treasure
Publisher: Time/Life Books, Inc.

121
Book
Artist: **Warren Linn**
Art Director: Ron Villani
Title: Yearbook of Science and the Future
Publisher: Encyclopaedia Britannica

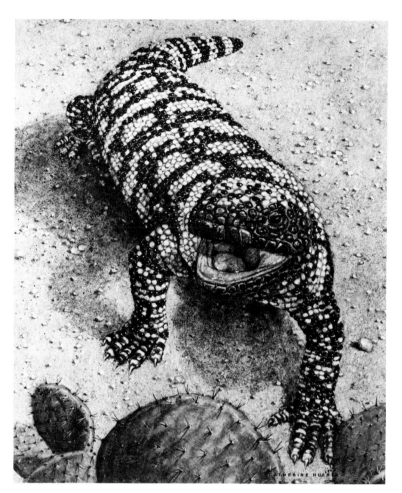

122
Editorial
Artist: **Catherine Huerta**
Art Director: Audrey Perrella/Dale Moyer
Publication: Scholastic Science World

123
Institutional
Artist: **Michael David Brown**
Art Director: Michael David Brown

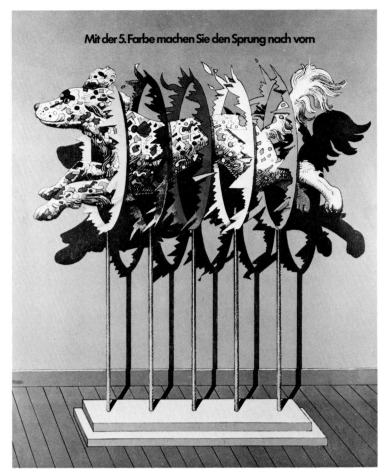

124
Advertising
Artist: **Milton Glaser**
Art Director: Robert Putz
Client: Werbeagentor Robert Putz

125
Institutional
Artist: **Charles Lilly**
Art Director: Ed Bunch/Bob Curry
Agency: D'Arcy MacManus & Masius
Client: Budweiser Brewing Co.

126
Institutional
Artist: **Ray Ameijide**
Art Director: Joe Landi
Agency: Landi & Handler Design, Inc.
Client: Roerig-Pfizer

127
Institutional
Artist: **Ray Ameijide**
Art Director: Joe Landi
Agency: Landi & Handler Design, Inc.
Client: Roerig-Pfizer

128
Advertising
Artist: **George Jurij Zebot**
Art Director: Douglas Hoppe Stone
Agency: Douglas Stone & Associates
Client: AMF Voit/Fernando Henriques

129
Institutional
Artist: **Bill Chambers**
Art Director: Bill Chambers
Client: Creative Source

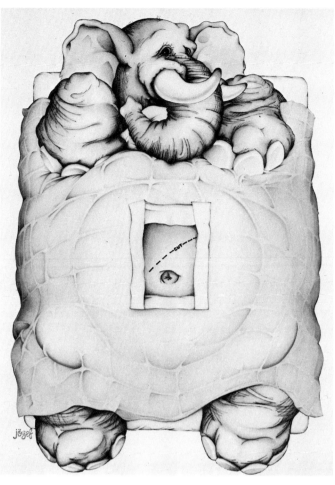

130
Institutional
Artist: **Jözef Sumichrast**
Art Director: Don Moravick
Client: Richard Allen

131
Advertising
Artist: **David Wilcox**
Art Director: Elena Pavlov
Client: CBS Records

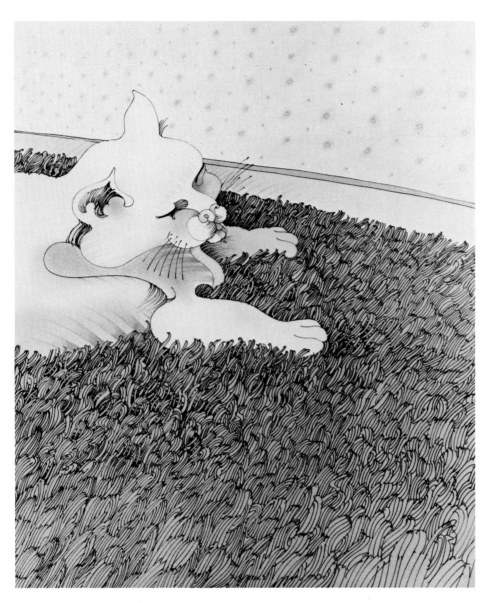

132
Institutional
Artist: **Don Weller**
Art Director: Don Weller
Agency: The Weller Institute for the Cure of Des
Client: Standard Brands   Paint Co.

133
TV/Film
Artist: **Bob Peluce**
Director: Bob Kurtz
Producer: Loraine Roberts
Production Company: Kurtz & Friends
Client: Heinz Canned Salads
Award for Excellence

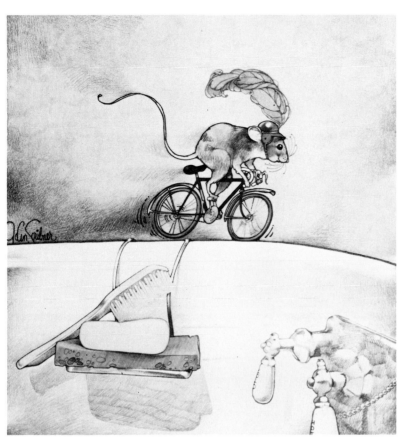

134
Book
Artist: **Joanne Scribner**
Art Director: Bruce W. Hall
Title: The Champion of Merrimack County
Publisher: Dell Publishing Co., Inc.

135
Advertising
Artist: **Karen Beckhardt**
Art Director: Katrinka Blickle
Client: Arista Records, Inc.

136
Book
Artist: **Leo & Diane Dillon**
Art Director: Doris Janowitz
Title: A Swiftly Tilting Planet
Publisher: Farrar, Straus & Giroux, Inc.

137
Advertising
Artist: **Bill Miller**
Art Director: Bruno Ruegg
Agency: Sieber & McIntyre Inc.
Client: General Diagnostics

Season's Greetings
from CBS◉

138
TV/Film
Artist: **Alice Campbell**
Art Director: Bill Snyder/Herman Aronson/
Alice Campbell
Producer: Jack Zander/Mark Zander
Production Co.: Zander's Animation Parlour
Client: CBS Television Network

139
Institutional
Artist: **Steven Saylor**
Art Director: Steven Saylor
Agency: Studios B.A. Butterbread
Client: Pomegranate

140
Institutional
Artist: **Leo & Diane Dillon**
Art Director: Leo & Diane Dillon
Client: Cathcart Gallery

141
Institutional
Artist: **Katrina Taylor**
Art Director: Richard Leberson/Iraj Naderi
Client: Facopa

142
Editorial
Artist: **Wilson McLean**
Art Director: Richard Gangel
Publication: Sports Illustrated

143
Advertising
Artist: **Wilson McLean**
Art Director: Peter Scavuzzo

144
Institutional
Artist: **Shelley Freshman**
Art Director: Shelley Freshman
Client: Multigrafiks

145
Book
Artist: **Jerry Pinkney**
Art Director: Lucy Bitzer
Title: Ji-Nongo Nongo
Publisher: Four Winds Press

146
Editorial
Artist: **Bob Kuhn**
Art Director: Victor J. Closi
Publication: Field & Stream Magazine

147
Institutional
Artist: **Hodges Soileau**
Art Director: John Scavnicky
Agency: Dixon & Eaton
Client: Diamond Shamrock

148
Institutional
Artist: **William Ersland**
Art Director: Gary Kelley
Agency: Hellman Design Associates
Client: Hellman Design Associates

149
TV/Film
Artist: **Bob Peluce**
Director: Bob Kurtz
Producer: Loraine Roberts
Production Company: Kurtz & Friends
Client: Chevron USA
Award for Excellence

150
Advertising
Artist: **Danny Wong/Christian Piper**
Art Director: Ed Lee
Client: CBS Records

151
Advertising
Artist: **Don Ivan Punchatz**
Art Director: William A. Schilling
Client: Smith, Kline & French Laboratories

152
Editorial
Artist: **Robert E. Hynes**
Art Director: Howard E. Paine
Publication: National Geographic

153
Institutional
Artist: **Mark English**
Art Director: James Wilkins
Agency: William F. Finn & Associates
Client: IMCO Services
Award for Excellence

DON'T FORGET THE COW
THE SOW AND THE HEN

CITIZENS
NATIONAL BANK
HENDERSON, TEXAS

154
Institutional
Artist: **Sandy Huffaker**
Art Director: Sandy Huffaker

155
Institutional
Artist: **Sandy Huffaker**
Art Director: Sandy Huffaker

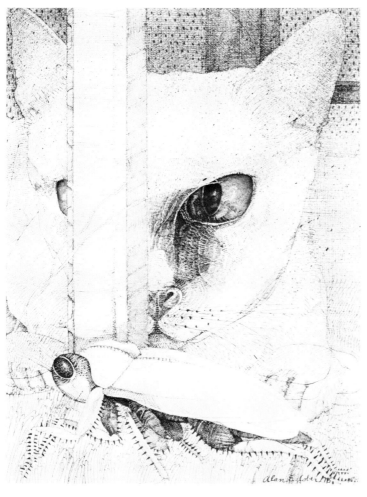

156
Editorial
Artist: **Alan E. Cober**
Art Director: Richard Becker
Publication: New Times Magazine

157
Editorial
Artist: **Ted CoConis**
Art Director: Bruce Danbrot/Don Adamec
Publication: Ladies' Home Journal

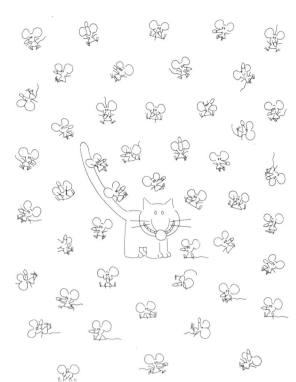

158
Institutional
Artist: **Bill Brewer**
Art Director: Bill Brewer
Client: Hallmark Cards

159
Institutional
Artist: **Harry Brown**
Art Director: Bill Brewer
Client: Hallmark Cards

160
Book
Artist: **Miki McCarron**
Art Director: Gordon Fisher
Publisher: The Franklin Library

161
Editorial
Artist: **Don Weller**
Art Director: Richard Coyne
Publication: CA Magazine

162
Advertising
Artist: **Carol Wald**
Art Director: Carol Wald

163
Advertising
Artist: **Bruce Wolfe**
Art Director: Bruce Wolfe
Client: Portal Publications

164
Editorial
Artist: **Kinuko Craft**
Art Director: Arthur Paul/Kerig Pope
Publication: Playboy Magazine

MERLIN & THE SNAKE'S EGG

Poems by Leslie Norris / Illustrated by Ted Lewin

165
Book
Artist: **Ted Lewin**
Art Director: Barbara Hennessy
Title: Merlin & The Snake's Egg
Publisher: The Viking Press

166
Institutional
Artist: **Paul Melia**
Art Director: Kay Timmons
Client: Good Samaritan Hospital

167
Editorial
Artist: **James C. Christensen**
Art Director: Preston Heiselt
Publication: New Era Magazine

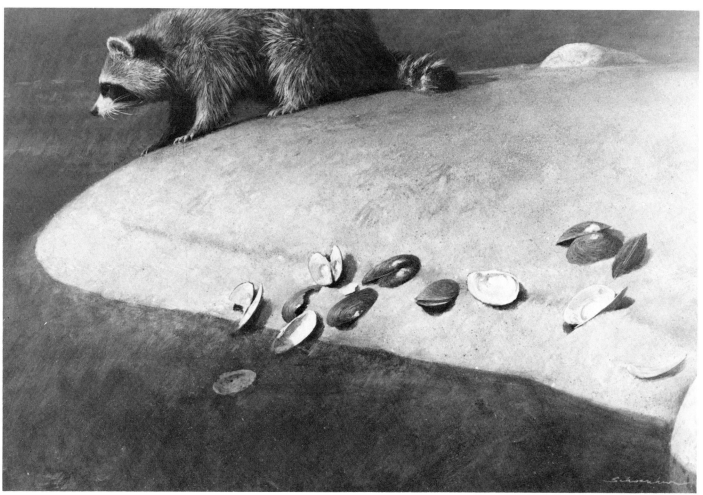

168
Institutional
Artist: **John Schoenherr**
Art Director: John Schoenherr
Client: Greenwich Workshop

169
Institutional
Artist: **Ivan Powell**
Art Director: Ivan Powell
Client: Glundal Color

170
Book
Artist: **Sandy Kossin**
Art Director: Leonard Leone
Title: The Life & Extraordinary
     Adventures of Pvt. Ivan Chonkea
Publisher: Bantam Books, Inc

171
Editorial
Artist: **Ed Soyka**
Art Director: Gordon Mortensen
Publication: Politics Today Magazine

172
Book
Artist: **Carl Lundgren**
Art Director: Frank Kozelek, Jr.
Title: Year's Finest Fantasy
Publisher: Berkley Publishing Corp.

173
Book
Artist: **Jim Conahan**
Art Director: Lydia Halverson/Hal Kearney
Title: The Faerie Queene
Publisher: Scott, Foresman & Company

174
Institutional
Artist: **Ray Ameijide**
Art Director: Tom Taylor/Gene Eggleston
Client: ARMCO Steel

175
Advertising
Artist: **Robert Heindel**
Art Director: Jim Bonner
Agency: Jim Bonner Advertising Art
Client: David M. Kleck & Associates

176
Editorial
Artist: **Roy Andersen**
Art Director: Howard E. Paine
Publication: National Geographic

Tyrannosaurus

177
Advertising
Artist: **Arnold Varga**
Art Director: Elmer Pizzi
Agency: Gray & Rogers, Inc.
Client: Grit

178
Institutional
Artist: **Catherine Huerta**
Art Director: Elmer Pizzi
Agency: Gray & Rogers, Inc.
Client: Grit-National Small Town Weekly

179
Institutional
Artist: **Bob Radigan**
Art Director: Bob Radigan

180
Advertising
Artist: **Linda Gist**
Art Director: Elmer Pizzi
Agency: Gray & Rogers, Inc.
Client: Grit

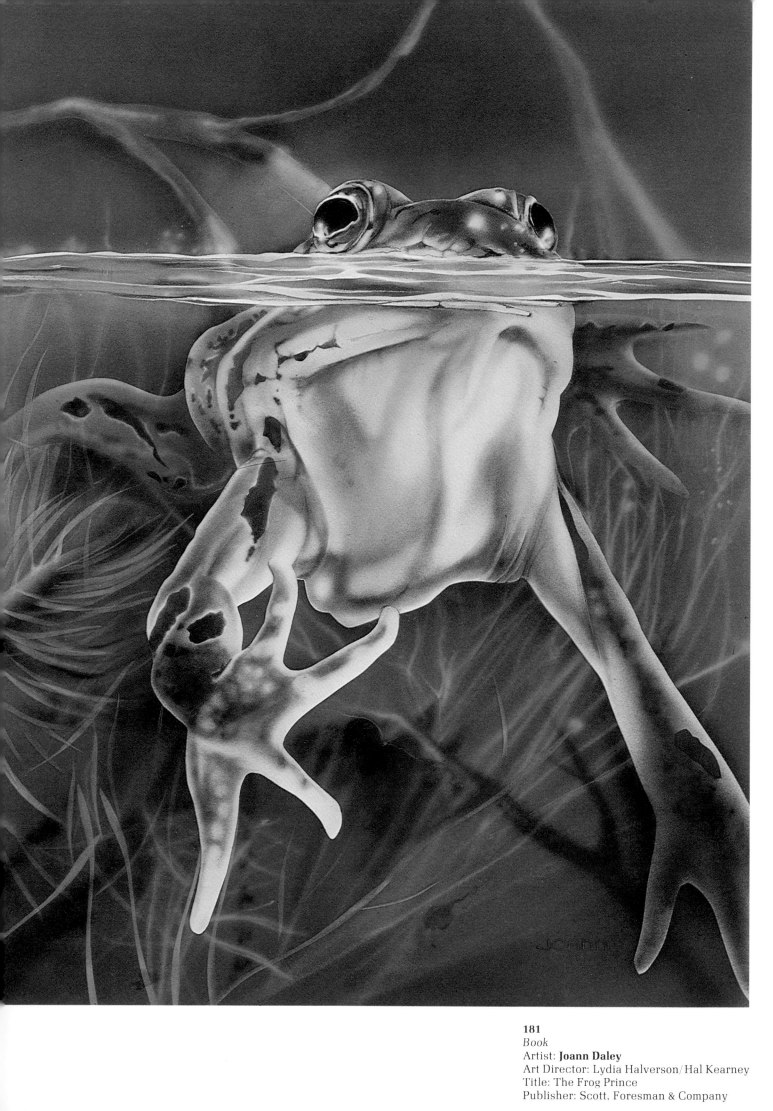

181
Book
Artist: **Joann Daley**
Art Director: Lydia Halverson/Hal Kearney
Title: The Frog Prince
Publisher: Scott, Foresman & Company

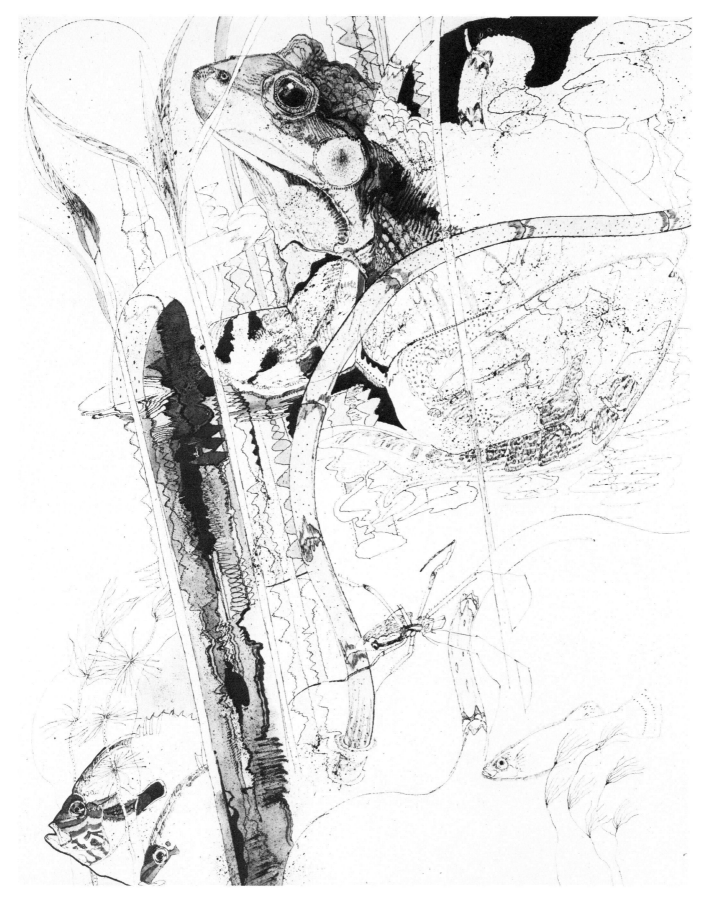

182
Institutional
Artist: **Jack Unruh**
Art Director: David Clark
Agency: Reflections
Client: Altosid

183
Advertising
Artist: **Jack Unruh**
Art Director: Chris Hill
Agency: Loucks Atelier
Client: United Gas

184
Advertising
Artist: **Jack Unruh**
Art Director: David Clark
Agency: Reflections
Client: Altosid

185
Institutional
Artist: **Jack Unruh**
Art Director: David Clark
Agency: Reflections
Client: Altosid

186
Advertising
Artist: **Richard Hess/Mark Hess**
Art Director: Brooke Kenney
Agency: Martin/Williams Advertising
Client: Minnesota Zoological Society

187
Institutional
Artist: **Jackie L. W. Geyer**
Art Director: Jeffrey G. Boyd
Agency: PPG Industries, Inc.
Client: PPG Foundation/Carnegie Museum
of Natural History

188
Book
Artist: **Richard Hess/Mark Hess**
Art Director: Lidia Ferrara
Title: A Species of Eternity
Publisher: Alfred A. Knopf, Inc.

John Muir

189
Institutional
Artist: **Larry Winborg**
Art Director: Larry Winborg
Agency: Winborg & Winborg
Client: Mountain Graphics

190
Book
Artist: **Ted Lewin**
Art Director: Soren Noring
Title: Prisoner at War
Publisher: Reader's Digest

191
Institutional
Artist: **David McCall Johnston**
Art Director: Keith English/Jaime Mas
Client: The Franklin Mint

192
Book
Artist: **Lucinda McQueen**
Art Director: Lucinda McQueen

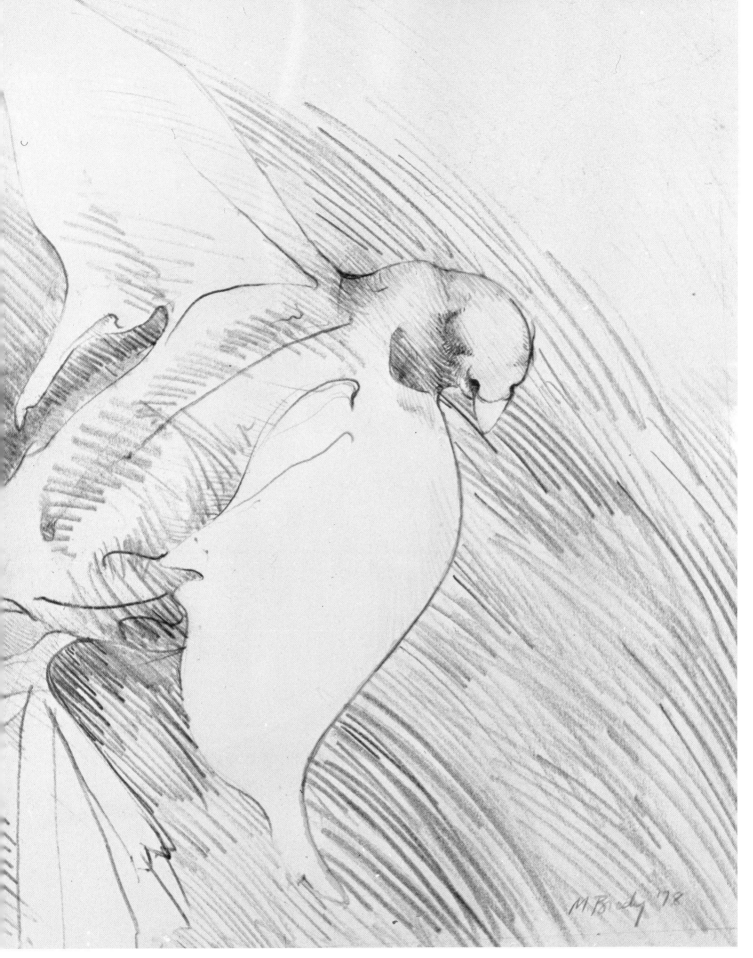

193
Book
Artist: **Marion Brody**
Art Director: Lawrence Levy/Hal Kearney
Title: Poetry—Unit 4
Publisher: Scott, Foresman & Company

194
Advertising
Artist: **Murray Tinkelman**
Art Director: Murray Tinkelman

195
Advertising
Artist: **Murray Tinkelman**
Art Director: Murray Tinkelman

196
Book
Artist: **Edward Koren**
Art Director: Janet Townsend
Title: Dragons Hate to be Discreet
Publisher: Alfred A. Knopf, Inc.

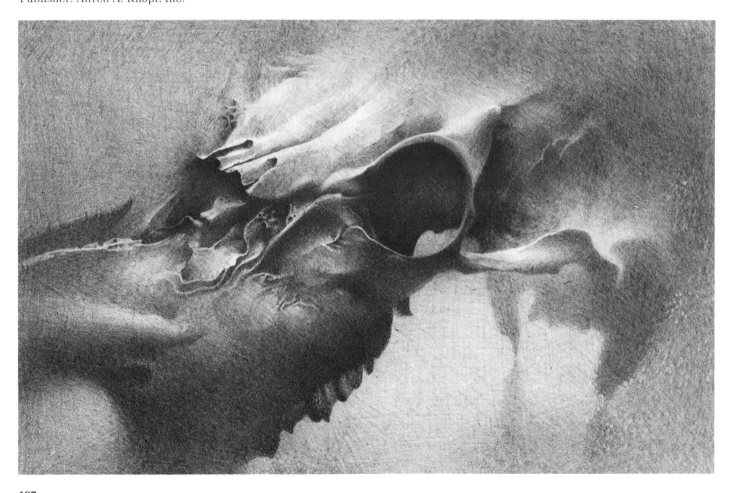

197
Book
Artist: **Jack Endewelt**
Art Director: Jack Endewelt

198
Institutional
Artist: **Simms Taback**
Art Director: Carol Carson
Client: Scholastic Magazines, Inc.

199
Book
Artist: **David Betts Garland**
Art Director: David Betts Garland
Title: Oldest Man Understands
Publisher: Chair Books

200
Book
Artist: **Jerry Podwil**
Art Director: Milton Charles
Title: Young Torless
Publisher: Pocket Books

201
Advertising
Artist: **Michael Knigin**
Art Director: Michael Knigin
Client: Think Group

202
Institutional
Artist: **Michael David Brown**
Art Director: Michael David Brown

203
Book
Artist: **Bernard Fuchs**
Art Director: Gordon Fisher
Publisher: The Franklin Library

204
Book
Artist: **Bernard Fuchs**
Art Director: Gordon Fisher
Publisher: The Franklin Library

205
Editorial
Artist: **Barron Storey**
Art Director: William A. Motta
Publication: Road & Track Magazine

ILLUSTRATION BY BARRON STOREY

206
Editorial
Artist: **Daniel Schwartz**
Art Director: Bruce Blair
Publication: Human Nature

207
Book
Artist: **Stan Hunter**
Art Director: Gordon Fisher
Title: Devil's Disciple
Publisher: The Franklin Library

208
Book
Artist: **Stan Hunter**
Art Director: Gordon Fisher
Title: Devil's Disciple
Publisher: The Franklin Library
Award for Excellence

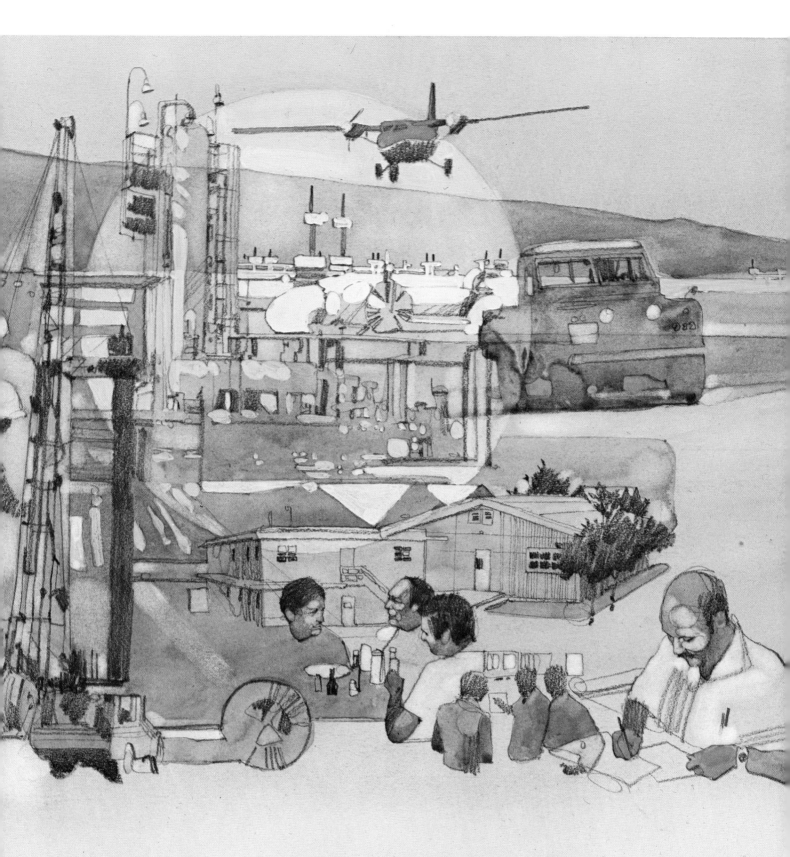

209
Editorial
Artist: **Randall McKissick**
Art Director: Stan Corfman
Publication: Marathon World

210
Advertising
Artist: **Paul Sachtleben**
Art Director: Paul Sachtleben

211
TV/Film
Artist: **Paul Melia**
Art Director: John Buchanan
Agency: Phil Office Associates
Client: Pacific Telephone Co.

212
Institutional
Artist: **Ruth Brunner-Strosser**
Art Director: Ruth Brunner-Strosser

213
Book
Artist: **Allan Mardon**
Art Director: Soren Noring
Title: Running for President
Publisher: Reader's Digest

214
Institutional
Artist: **Edward Sorel**
Art Director: Lidia Ferrara
Client: AIGA Book Clinic

215
Institutional
Artist: **Dick Lubey**
Art Director: Dick Lubey
Client: Carl Zollo

216
Advertising
Artist: **Artie Horowitz**
Art Director: Martha Savitsky
Client: School of Visual Arts

217
Advertising
Artist: **Steven Hofheimer**
Art Director: Jim Witker
Client: Tavistock

218
Editorial
Artist: **Lloyd K. Townsend**
Art Director: Howard E. Paine
Publication: National Geographic

219
Advertising
Artist: **Alan Magee**
Art Director: Alan Magee
Client: A & M Records

220
Book
Artist: **John Berkey**
Art Director: Gordon Fisher
Title: Winesburg, Ohio
Publisher: The Franklin Library

221
Book
Artist: **Bernard Colonna**
Art Director: Diana Hrisinko
Title: Grandpa and Me
Publisher: Charles Scribner's Sons

222
Book
Artist: **John Berkey**
Art Director: Gordon Fisher
Title: Winesburg, Ohio
Publisher: The Franklin Library

223
Editorial
Artist: **Paul Giovanopoulos**
Art Director: Carveth Kramer
Publication: Psychology Today

224
Editorial
Artist: **Julian Allen**
Art Director: Bob Priest
Publication: Weekend Magazine

225
Institutional
Artist: **James Franklin Berge**
Art Director: James Franklin Berge
Client: Gregg Co., Ltd.

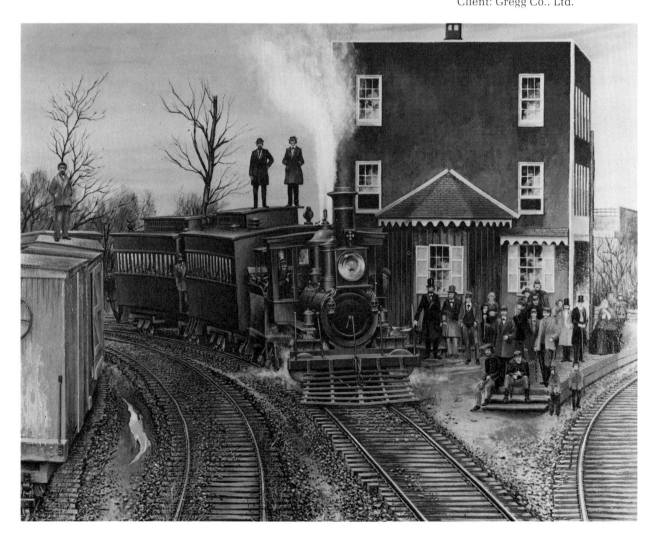

226
Book
Artist: **Ed Soyka**
Art Director: Milton Charles
Title: Two Worlds of Childhood, US-USSR
Publisher: Pocket Books

227
Editorial
Artist: **Fred Otnes**
Art Director: Joseph Connolly
Publication: Boys' Life Magazine

228
Institutional
Artist: **Charles McVicker**
Art Director: Charles McVicker

229
Institutional
Artist: **Albino Hinojosa**
Art Director: Albino Hinojosa
Client: Ruston State Bank

230
Book
Artist: **Joe Ciardiello**
Art Director: Gordon Fisher/Jack Tauss
Title: The Magic Mountain
Publisher: The Franklin Library

231
Book
Artist: **Mark Bellerose**
Art Director: Gordon Fisher
Title: Beggarman, Thief
Publisher: The Franklin Library

232
Advertising
Artist: **Steve Takenaga**
Art Director: Steve Takenaga
Client: J. Walter Thompson Co. — Detroit

233
Advertising
Artist: **Sean Daly**
Art Director: Sean Daly

234
Institutional
Artist: **Paul Melia**
Art Director: Gene Vanard
Client: The General Tire & Rubber Co.

235
Editorial
Artist: **William A. Motta**
Art Director: William A. Motta

236
Institutional
Artist: **David Grove**
Art Director: Carol Taylor
Agency: Corporate Graphics
Client: Consolidated Freightways Inc

237
Advertising
Artist: **Greg Harris**
Art Director: Greg harris

238
Advertising
Artist: **David Kimble**
Art Director: Ron Wolin
Agency: Grey Advertising
Client: American Honda Motor Co., Inc.

239
Editorial
Artist: **Steve Karchin**
Art Director: Alice Degenhardt
Publication: Creative Living Magazine

240
Advertising
Artist: **Joe Isom**
Art Director: Steve Mangan
Agency: Mangan-Rains-Ginnaven Associates
Client: Win Paul Rockefeller/Winrock Farms

241
Institutional
Artist: **Howard Koslow**
Art Director: W. K. Plummer
Agency: The Franklin Mint
Client: Postmasters of America

242
Institutional
Artist: **Gary Kelley**
Art Director: Gary Kelley
Client: Hellman Design Associates

243
Institutional
Artist: **Michael David Brown**
Art Director: Michael David Brown
Client: Foxhall Editions

244
Editorial
Artist: **George Sottung**
Art Director: George Sottung

245
Book
Artist: **Chris Spollen**
Art Director: Chris Spollen
Title: Solictious Lull
Publisher: Moonlight Press

246
Editorial
Artist: **Harry J. Schaare**
Art Director: Harry J. Schaare

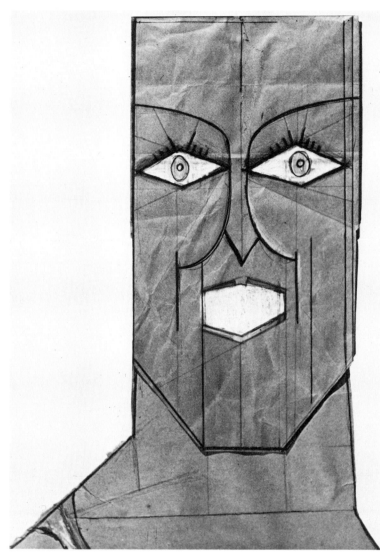

247
Book
Artist: **Saul Steinberg**
Art Director: R. D. Scudellari
Title: Saul Steinberg
Publisher: Alfred A. Knopf, Inc.

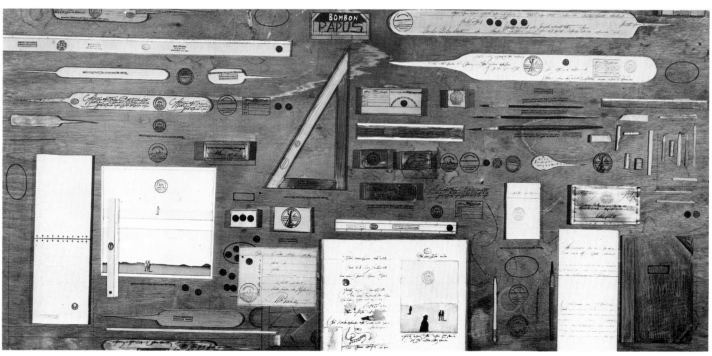

248
Book
Artist: **Saul Steinberg**
Art Director: R. D. Scudellari
Title: Saul Steinberg
Publisher: Alfred A. Knopf, Inc.

249
Advertising
Artist: **Miki McCarron**
Art Director: Ron Vereltzis
Client: CIBA-Geigy Corp.

250
Institutional
Artist: **Norman Walker**
Art Director: Terry Rose
Agency: Wesson & Warhaftig, Inc.
Client: Schering Corp.

251
Book
Artist: **John Berkey**
Art Director: Barbara Bertoli
Title: Interstellar Travel
Publisher: Avon Books

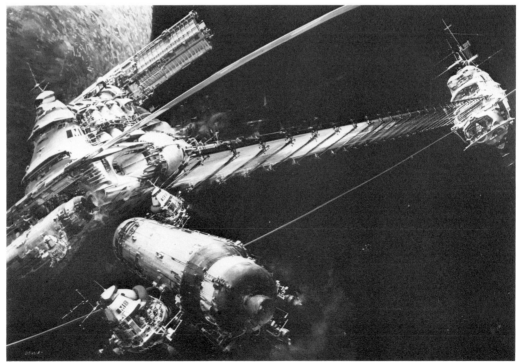

252
Advertising
Artist: **John Berkey**
Art Director: Clarence Weight/
Michael Altizer
Agency: J.P. Hogan & Co.
Client: Martin Processing Inc.

253
Editorial
Artist: **Shusei Nagaoka**
Art Director: Robert P. Ericksen
Publication: Starlog/Future Magazine

254
Institutional
Artist: **Joseph M. Ovies**
Art Director: J.C. Prain/Pat Pantonini
Client: WABC Musicradio 77

255
Institutional
Artist: **Stephen Hunter**
Art Director: Seth G. Huntington
Agency: Brown & Bigelow
Client: Nekoosa Paper Company

256
Institutional
Artist: **Rick MacDonald**
Art Director: J. Dooley/D. Arnold
Agency: Creative Services
Client: American Aviation Underwriters

257
Editorial
Artist: **William A. Motta**
Art Director: William A. Motta

258
Advertising
Artist: **Robert M. Cunningham**
Art Director: Robert M. Cunningham

259
TV/Still
Artist: **Barbara Goodman**
Art Director: Joe Sparkman
Client: WLS-TV

260
Advertising
Artist: **Walter Rane**
Art Director: Walter Rane
Client: David Hankins

261
Institutional
Artist: **Larry Winborg**
Art Director: Larry Winborg
Agency: Winborg & Winborg
Client: Mountain Graphics

262
Institutional
Artist: **Stan Hunter**
Art Director: Peter Bevacqua
Agency: N.W. Ayer ABH International
Client: United States Army

263
Editorial
Artist: **Daniel Maffia**
Art Director: Michael Brock
Publication: Oui Magazine

264
Book
Artist: **Daniel Maffia**
Art Director: Lidia Ferrara
Title: Wuthering Heights
Publisher: Alfred A. Knopf, Inc.

265
Institutional
Artist: **Robert Kinyon**
Art Director: Peter Bevacqua
Publication: N.W. Ayer ABH International
Client: United States Army

266
Editorial
Artist: **John Collier**
Art Director: Maxine Davidowitz
Publication: Redbook Magazine

267
Advertising
Artist: **Don Daily**
Art Director: Elmer Pizzi
Agency: Gray & Rogers, Inc.
Client: Weyerhaeuser Paper Division

268
Book
Artist: **David Grove**
Art Director: Don Smith
Title: The Subterraneans
Publisher: Ballantine Books, Inc.

269
Institutional
Artist: **Jim Butcher**
Art Director: Peter Bevacqua
Agency: N.W. Ayer ABH International
Client: United States Army

270
Institutional
Artist: **Jerry Pinkney**
Art Director: Lee Estes
Agency: N.W. Ayers ABH International
Client: R.O.T.C.

271
Editorial
Artist: **Bernard Fuchs**
Art Director: Richard Gangel
Publication: Sports Illustrated

272
Institutional
Artist: **Gary Kelley**
Art Director: Gary Kelley
Client: Hellman Design Associates

273
Institutional
Artist: **Tony Eubanks**
Art Director: Tony Eubanks

274
Institutional
Artist: **Stan Hunter**
Art Director: Peter Bevacqua
Agency: N.W. Ayer AHB International
Client: United States Army

275
Book
Artist: **Norman Walker**
Art Director: Jim Plumeri
Title: American Indian
Publisher: New American Library

276
Book
Artist: **Bob Crofut**
Art Director: Bob Crofut

Yellowstone

277
Institutional
Artist: **Larry Winborg**
Art Director: Larry Winborg
Agency: Winborg & Winborg
Client: Mountain Graphics

278
Institutional
Artist: **Tony Eubanks**
Art Director: Tony Eubanks

279
Institutional
Artist: **Mike Eagle**
Art Director: Sande Bristol
Client: Aetna Life & Casualty Co.

280
Editorial
Artist: **Karmen Effenberger**
Art Director: Lee Gladish
Publication: Colorado Quarterly

281
Institutional
Artist: **Mike Eagle**
Art Director: Sande Bristol
Client: Aetna Life & Casualty Co.

282
Advertising
Artist: **Norman Walker**
Art Director: Dolores Gudzin
Client: NBC Television

283
Book
Artist: **Mark Hess**
Art Director: Lidia Ferrara
Title: Eagle Fur
Publisher: Alfred A. Knopf, Inc.

284
Advertising
Artist: **Cliff Condak**
Art Director: Paula Scher
Client: CBS Records

285
Advertising
Artist: **Jerry McDaniel**
Art Director: Jerry McDaniel
Agency: J. W. McDaniel Studio
Client: Churchill Downs

286
Institutional
Artist: **Linda Crockett-Hanzel**
Art Director: Linda Crockett-Hanzel

287
Book
Artist: **Jön Pickard**
Art Director: Jön Pickard/Ron Ketchum
Title: Chas. Quirt, Esq.
Publisher: Ron Ketchum & Associates

288
Book
Artist: **John Robinette**
Art Director: John Robinette

289
Institutional
Artist: **Walt Spitzmiller**
Art Director: Barry Newcomb
Agency: Newcomb House Design
Client: 7-Up Bottling Co.

290
Institutional
Artist: **Walt Spitzmiller**
Art Director: Walt Spitzmiller
Client: Payson Enterprise

291
Editorial
Artist: **William A. Harmuth**
Art Director: William A. Harmuth

292
Advertising
Artist: **Bart Forbes**
Art Director: Vince Maiello
Client: The Literary Guild

293
Editorial
Artist: **John Collier**
Art Director: Richard Gangel
Publication: Sports Illustrated

294
Editorial
Artist: **Sandy Huffaker**
Art Director: Richard Gangel
Publication: Sports Illustrated

295
TV/Still
Artist: **Bill Dula**
Art Director: Lee Stousland
Client: NBC Television

296
Institutional
Artist: **Scott Greer**
Art Director: Micheal Richards
Agency: University Graphic Design
Client: Division of Continuing Education
        University of Utah

297
Editorial
Artist: **Gerry Gersten**
Art Director: Richard Becker
Publication: New Times Magazine

298
Editorial
Artist: **Bernard Fuchs**
Art Director: Jerry Alten
Publication: TV Guide

299
Institutional
Artist: **Bill Nelson**
Art Director: Bill Nelson

300
Institutional
Artist: **Bob Lapsley**
Art Director: Bob Lapsley

301
Institutional
Artist: **Maurice Kennel**
Art Director: Maurice Kennel
Client: The Illustrators Workshop

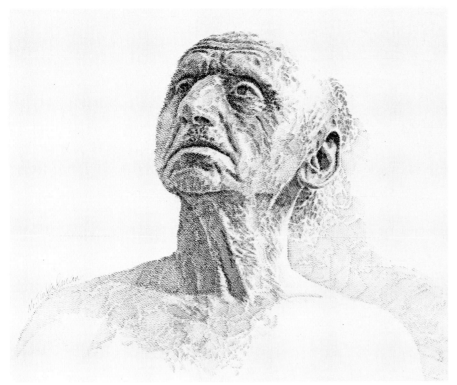

302
Book
Artist: **Murray Tinkelman**
Art Director: Milton Charles
Title: The Survivor
Publisher: Pocket Books

303
Editorial
Artist: **Robert Heindel**
Art Director: Richard Gangel
Publication: Sports Illustrated

R·GIUSTI

304
Editorial
Artist: **Robert Giusti**
Art Director: Jerry Alten
Publication: TV Guide

305
Editorial
Artist: **Walt Spitzmiller**
Art Director: Richard Gangel
Publication: Sports Illustrated

306
Editorial
Artist: **Reagan Wilson**
Art Director: Norm Shaffer
Publication: Playboy Magazine

307
Editorial
Artist: **David Grove**
Art Director: David Boss
Publication: PRO Magazine

308
Editorial
Artist: **Walt Spitzmiller**
Art Director: Pete Libby
Publication: Golf Digest

309
Editorial
Artist: **Fred Otnes**
Art Director: Richard Gangel
Publication: Sports Illustrated

310
Editorial
Artist: **Birney Lettick**
Art Director: Walter Bernard
Publication: Time Magazine

311
Editorial
Artist: **Robert M. Cunningham**
Art Director: Richard Gangel
Publication: Sports Illustrated

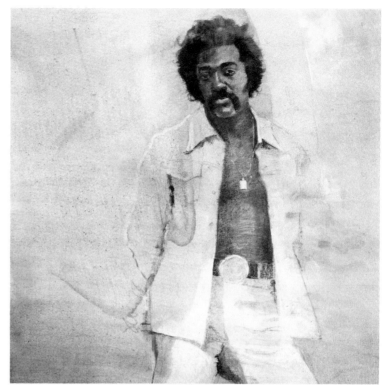

312
Institutional
Artist: **Bill James**
Art Director: Bill James

313
Advertising
Artist: **Peter Fiore**
Art Director: Bob Heimall
Agency: AGI
Client: T. K. Productions, Inc.

The downfall of a proud N.Y. high school

A teacher at Manhattan High, a vocational school on East 96th Street, chronicles its decline

by FOTINE NICHOLAS

To the joy of some and the cynical skepticism of certain other, worldly-wise students, it was announced last year that Manhattan Vocational-Technical High School, once an elementary school, later Hunter College High School, then a wartime vocational school with the descriptive name of Machine and Metal Trades High School, would be renovated and painted after a lapse of a quarter of a century.

For years rumors had abounded that the H-shaped academic building, one of the uglier school buildings in New York, would be abandoned for a new one to be built on Park Ave. Other rumors were that a new building would be erected on the playground on the north side of the street, or that the school would disappear and the students would be scattered among schools in areas with less real-estate potential.

Many parts of the turn-of-the-century red brick building look battle-scarred. Classroom walls are peeling, ceilings seem in danger of imminent collapse, parts of staircase walls have been knocked out, students' desks have been gouged, teachers' desks and chairs are traps for tragic clothing and instincts. The so-called teachers' lounge, a former storeroom, seems a leftover from some long-forgotten war. But human beings tend to be hopeful and year after year the word has gone around. This is the year everything will be made over. Soon we may even have a real gymnasium again.

Manhattan High straddles E. 96th St. just off the East River Drive. Of a Friday afternoon, as cars crowd into the street on their way to a country weekend, it often resembles the Long Island Expressway. The main building is at the northernmost edge of Yorkville and the "new" shop building (of 1843) vintage) opposite is at the beginning of East Harlem. The school's ethnic mix might be termed Harlem, East Harlem, with a bit of Yorkville, lower East Side and Chinatown thrown in. Twenty-five years ago, like the surrounding area, Machine and Metal Trades, or MMT, was primarily a "Catholic" school, populated for the most part by students of Irish and Italian extraction. One of the better vocational high schools, it had provided skilled labor for wartime factories, capable craftsmen for industry and technical students who went on to industrial arts high schools.

It was a school where white shirts and ties were worn at formal weekly assemblies, where the school song was sung with enthusiasm if not style; where the English department was headed by Waspish, dignified ladies with 19th-century ideas; where the principal, who was to rule almost dictatorially for 20 years, never took a day of sick leave. Later at his retirement it was rumored that he had turned over his sick leave pay to the Board of Education.

Such was MMT — before the union, the strikes, the drugs, Vietnam, teacher injuries, walkouts, before the almost-daily classroom fights, the stress and strife and confusion, the bitterness, sullenness and cynicism. Those were the days when a new female teacher, warned by her mother to be careful with "those rough boys," walked down the long, narrow halls and looked through open doors into crowded classrooms that seemed to be a teacher's heaven.

It was a time when the principal refused to allow mention of a certain student in the school newspaper. The student was a promising Golden Gloves boxer who would later become moderately famous. "We don't want items like that getting publicity and giving the school a bad name" was the explanation. Carlos Ortiz had done nothing more than cut a few classes.

It was a time when the track team was producing outstanding runners, including John Carlos, an Olympic medalist; the gymnastics class compared favorably with European models, and the baseball team won a borough championship. The honor society was active and the student court was strong. MMT-MVT was not an elite school. In some ways it was a rough school. But it was producing a few engineers and some teachers and many outstand-

continued on page 20

314
Editorial
Artist: **Alan Reingold**
Art Director: Bob Clive
Publication: Sunday News Magazine

315
Advertising
Artist: **Robert Weaver**
Art Director: John Berg
Client: CBS Records

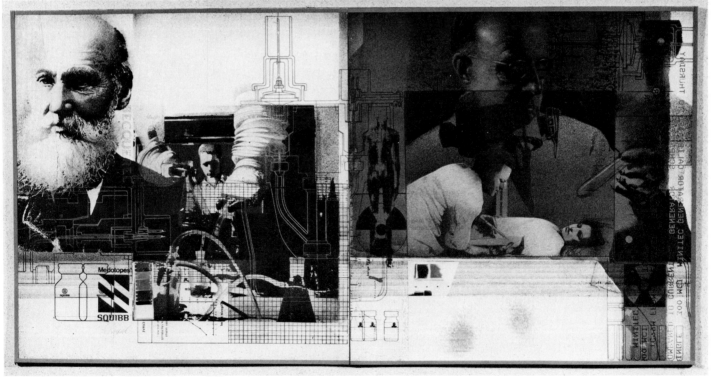

316
Institutional
Artist: **Richard Krepel**
Art Director: Tony Pozsonyi
Agency: Pozsonyi Design
Client: Squibb & Sons

317
Advertising
Artist: **Norman Orr**
Art Director: Norman Orr

SAN FRANCISCO BALLET

NUTCRACKER

318
Editorial
Artist: **Jeff Cummins**
Art Director: Michael Brock/George Kenton
Publication: Oui Magazine

319
Advertising
Artist: **James McMullan**
Art Director: Paula Scher
Client: Columbia Records

320
Editorial
Artist: **Julian Allen**
Art Director: Michael Brock
Publication: Oui Magazine

321
Book
Artist: **Miriam Schottland**
Art Director: Hugh O'Neil
Title: The Killing Zone
Publisher: W. W. Norton & Co., Inc.

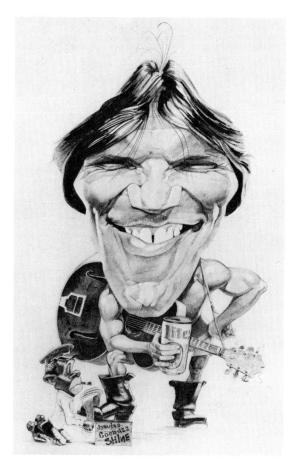

322
Institutional
Artist: **Maurice Lewis**
Art Director: Maurice Lewis
Client: Hodges Soileau

323
Advertising
Artist: **David Wilcox**
Art Director: Paula Scher
Client: CBS Records

324
Institutional
Artist: **Gary Ciccarelli**
Art Director: Jim Prain
Agency: J.C. Prain & Associates
Client: WABC Radio

325
Advertising
Artist: **Doug Johnson**
Art Director: Joseph Stelmach
Client: RCA Records

326
Advertising
Artist: **Bob Ziering**
Art Director: Howard Fritzon/Ron Kellum
Client: Arista Records, Inc.

327
Institutional
Artist: **John Alcorn**
Art Director: Susan Lyster
Agency: McCaffrey & McCall, Inc.
Client: Exxon

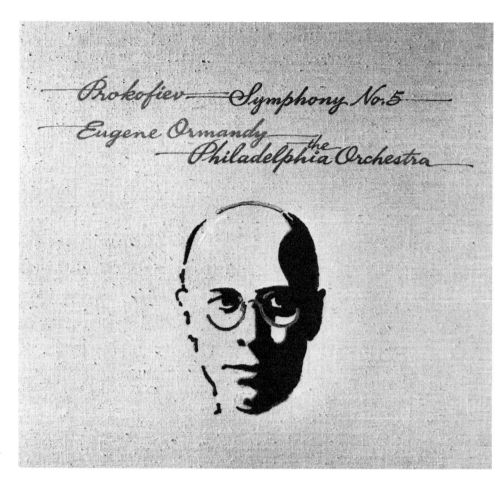

328
Advertising
Artist: **Joseph Stelmach**
Art Director: Joseph Stelmach
Client: RCA Records

329
Advertising
Artist: **Richard Sparks**
Art Director: Dick Smith/Acey Lehman
Client: RCA Records

330
Advertising
Artist: **Paul Davis**
Art Director: Silas H. Rhodes
Client: School of Visual Arts

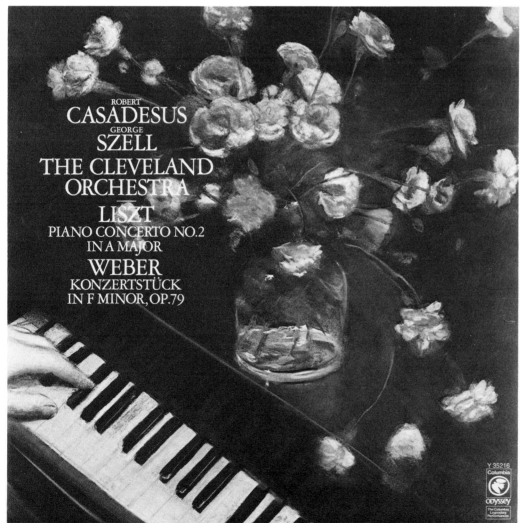

331
Advertising
Artist: **John Collier**
Art Director: Henrietta Condak
Client: CBS Records

332
Institutional
Artist: **Rick MacDonald**
Art Director: Bernard Fuchs/Bob Peak

333
Advertising
Artist: **Cliff Condak**
Art Director: Henrietta Condak
Client: CBS Records

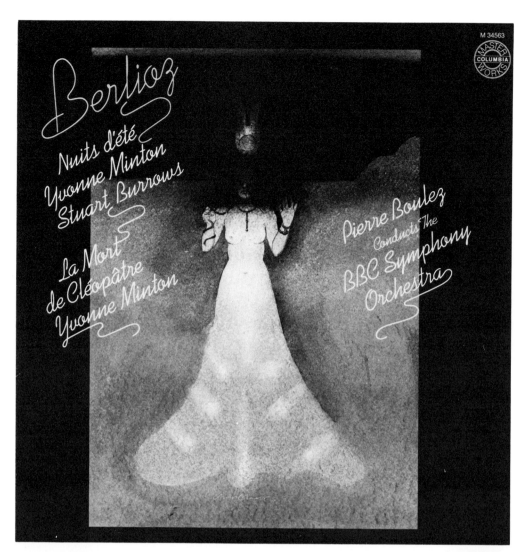

334
Advertising
Artist: **Milton Glaser**
Art Director: Henrietta Condak
Client: Columbia Records
Award for Excellence

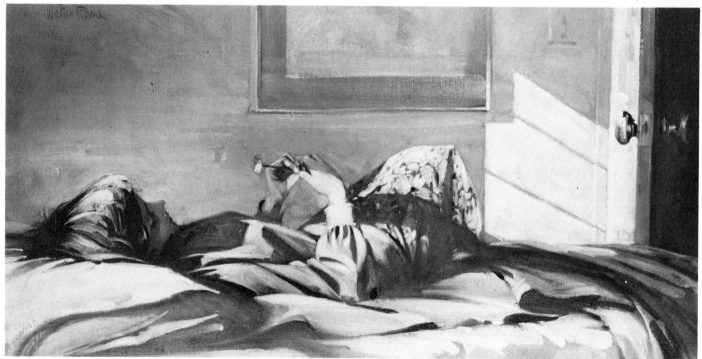

335
Institutional
Artist: **Walter Rane**
Art Director: Walter Rane
Client: David Hankins

336
Advertising
Artist: **Joseph Stelmach**
Art Director: Joseph Stelmach
Client: RCA Records

337
Institutional
Artist: **Skip Liepke**
Art Director: Skip Liepke

338
Advertising
Artist: **Robert Weaver**
Art Director: Ron Kellum
Client: Arista Records, Inc.

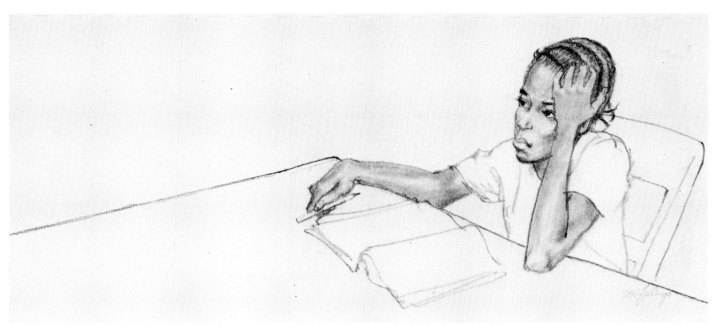

339
Book
Artist: **Tom Feelings**
Art Director: Atha Tehon
Title: Something On My Mind
Publisher: The Dial Press

340
Advertising
Artist: **Jeffrey Terreson**
Art Director: Dolores Gudzin
Client: NBC Television

341
Editorial
Artist: **Richard Sparks**
Art Director: Noel Werrett
Publication: Quest/78

342
Institutional
Artist: **Mike Hodges**
Art Director: Joseph Stelmach
Client: RCA Records

343
Advertising
Artist: **Patricia Dryden**
Art Director: Ron Kellum
Client: Arista Records

344
Advertising
Artist: **Steve Karchin**
Art Director: John Murello
Client: RCA Records

345
Advertising
Artist: **Jan Masters**
Art Director: Ron Kellum/Jan Masters
Client: Arista Records, Inc.

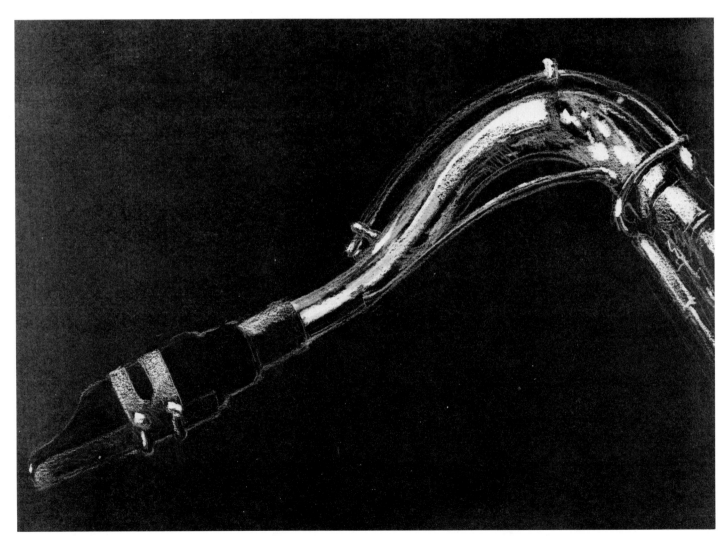

346
Advertising
Artist: **Thomas B. Allen**
Art Director: John Berg
Client: CBS Records

347
Advertising
Artist: **Edwin Herder**
Art Director: Ace Lehman/Dick Smith
Client: RCA Records

348
Advertising
Artist: **David Wilcox**
Art Director: Ron Coro/Johnny Lee
Client: Elektra/Asylum Records

349
Institutional
Artist: **Allen Welkis**
Art Director: Harry Sykora
Client: SONY Corp. of America

350
Institutional
Artist: **Barry Phillips**
Art Director: Dave Tougas
Client: Lucid Lines

351
Advertising
Artist: **Barry Phillips**
Art Director: Barry Phillips

352
Advertising
Artist: **Gerard Huerta**
Art Director: Ed Lee
Client: CBS Records

353
Editorial
Artist: **Charles Santore**
Art Director: Maxine Davidowitz
Publication: Redbook Magazine

354
Book
Artist: **Doug Johnson**
Art Director: James Plumeri
Title: Disco Fever
Publisher: New American Library

355
Advertising
Artist: **Seymour Chwast**
Art Director: Paula Scher
Client: CBS Records

356
Book
Artist: **Hilary Hayton**
Art Director/Editor: Jill Mackay
Publisher: Pan Books

357
Book
Artist: **Harvey Dinnerstein**
Art Director: Bob Fillie
Title: Artist at Work
Publisher: Watson-Guptill Publications

358
Advertising
Artist: **Mike Steirnagle/
Henry Martinez**
Art Director: Mike Steirnagle/
Henry Martinez
Agency: The Drawing Room
Client: Jonsil Rings

359
Advertising
Artist: **John Pirman**
Art Director: J. Charles Walker
Agency: Tarragon Graphics
Client: Tarragon Graphics

360
TV/Film
Artist: **Richard Tomlinson**
Art Director: Jerry Bailis
Client: WNEW-TV News

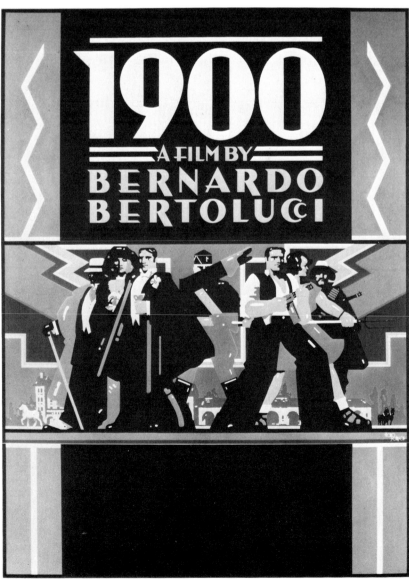

361
Advertising
Artist: **Doug Johnson**
Art Director: Doug Johnson
Agency: Rosebud Advertising
Client: Paramount Pictures

362
TV/Still
Artist: **Wendy M. Sawyer**
Art Director: Wendy M. Sawyer

363
Advertising
Artist: **Richard Hess**
Art Director: Paula Scher
Client: CBS Records

364
Book
Artist: **George Masi**
Art Director: Skip Sorvino
Title: The Mad Doctor
Publisher: Scholastic Magazines, Inc.

365
Book
Artist: **Terry Steadham**
Art Director: Dick Adelson
Title: Arthur C. Clarke
Publisher: Random House, Inc.

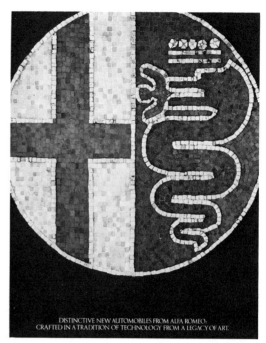

366
Editorial
Artist: **Dickran Palulian**
Art Director: Joe Brooks
Publication: Penthouse Magazine

367
Advertising
Artist: **John Klammer**
Art Director: David Corbett
Agency: Wunderman, Ricotta & Kline, Inc.
Client: Alfa-Romeo Corp.

368
Editorial
Artist: **Richard D. Harvey**
Art Director: Bruce Danbrot
Publication: Ladies' Home Journal

369
Institutional
Artist: **John Sposato**
Art Director: John Sposato
Client: Atwater Press

370
Institutional
Artist: **Larry McEntire**
Art Director: Michael Strickland
Agency: Michael Strickland Associates
Client: The Summit

371
Book
Artist: **Whole Hog Studio**
Art Director: Barbara Bertoli
Title: The Magic of Honey
Publisher: Avon Books

372
Institutional
Artist: **Richard Farrell**
Art Director: Gary Kelley
Agency: Hellman Design Associates
Client: Hellman Design Associates

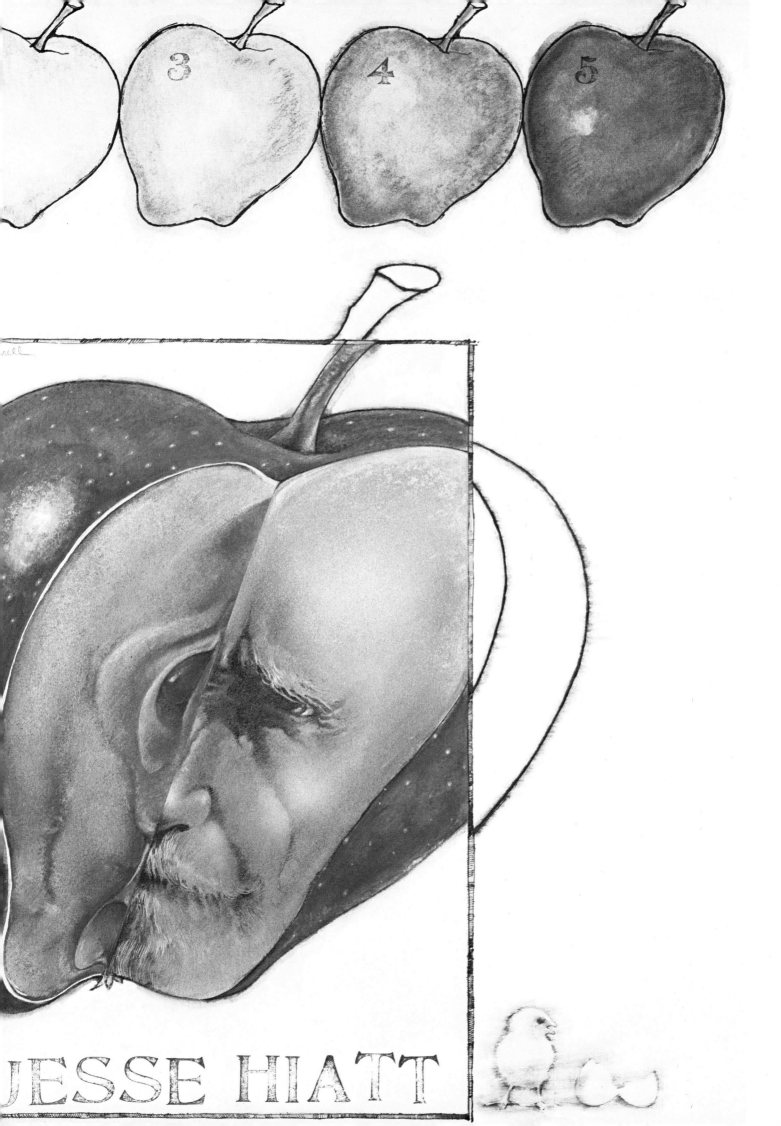

JESSE HIATT

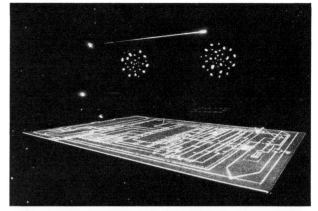

373
TV/Film
Artist: **Skip Ishii**
Art Director: Skip Ishii
Production Co.: Skip Ishii Productions, Inc.
Client: Hitachi Sales Corporation

374
Advertising
Artist: **Shusei Nagaoka**
Art Director: Ace Lehman/Shusei Nagaoka
Client: RCA Records

375
TV/Film
Artist: **Peter Lloyd**
Director: Bob Kurtz
Producer: Loraine Roberts
Production Co.: Kurtz & Friends
Client: Reynolds Aluminum

376
Book
Artist: **Dennis Luzak**
Art Director: Lem Rauk
Title: Second Sighting
Publisher: Jove Publications Inc.

377
Editorial
Artist: **Mark Alan Stamaty**
Art Director: George Delmerico
Publication: The Village Voice

378
Book
Artist: **Sal Catalano**
Art Director: Skip Sorvino
Title: Our Park
Publisher: Scholastic Magazines

379
Book
Artist: **David Grove**
Art Director: Don Smith
Title: The Consul's File
Publisher: Ballantine Books, Inc.

380
Editorial
Artist: **Barbara Higgins Bond**
Art Director: Edward L. Towles
Publication: Black Enterprise Magazine

The season for pears is upon us, and markets everywhere now carry most of these luscious varieties: the sweet and juicy Comice, a small, plump winter pear that ripens to yellow or bright red; the popular late-summer Bartlett, crunchy and delicious; fall's long-necked, russet-colored Bosc; and the Anjou, a fine-textured pear of freshest green that turns to golden-yellow. Pears are usually picked from the tree before they're ripe, so the ones you buy may need to rest at room temperature for a day or two until gentle pressure from your fingertips tells you they're ready for eating. And then—what lovely ways there are to use them! Suggestions for pies, cobblers and other treats begin on page 159.

381
Editorial
Artist: **Alan Magee**
Art Director: Al Grossman
Publication: McCall's Magazine

382
Editorial
Artist: **Richard Kimbrough**
Art Director: Richard Kimbrough

383
Institutional
Artist: **Joseph M. Ovies**
Art Director: J.C. Prain/Pat Pantonini
Client: WABC Musicradio/Coca Cola

384
Advertising
Artist: **Louise Scott**
Art Director: Louise Scott
Client: Hiro Sushi Restaurant

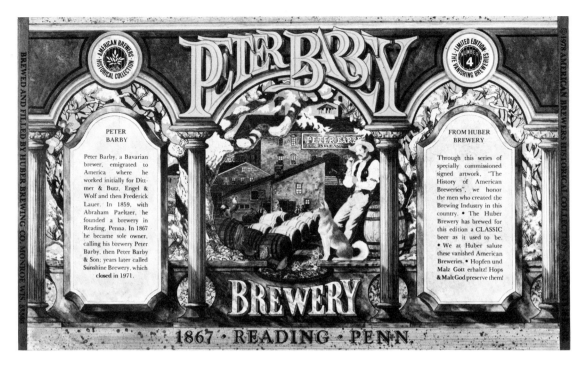

385
Institutional
Artist: **Steven R. Kidd**
Art Director: Gould Hulse
Client: American Brewers Historical Collection

386
Institutional
Artist: **Kirsten Soderlind**
Art Director: Kirsten Soderlind
Client: Britta Soderlind

387
Editorial
Artist: **Adolf Schaller**
Art Director: Robert P. Ericksen
Publication: Future/Starlog Magazine

388
Institutional
Artist: **Kirsten Soderlind**
Art Director: Chris Hill

389
Editorial
Artist: **Carol Inouye**
Art Director: Tom Reis
Publication: American Way Magazine

390
Advertising
Artist: **Carol Inouye**
Art Director: Phil Gips
Agency: Gips & Balkind Inc.
Client: Business Week

391
Editorial
Artist: **Gerald McConnell**
Art Director: Gerald McConnell
Publication: Mennen Corp.

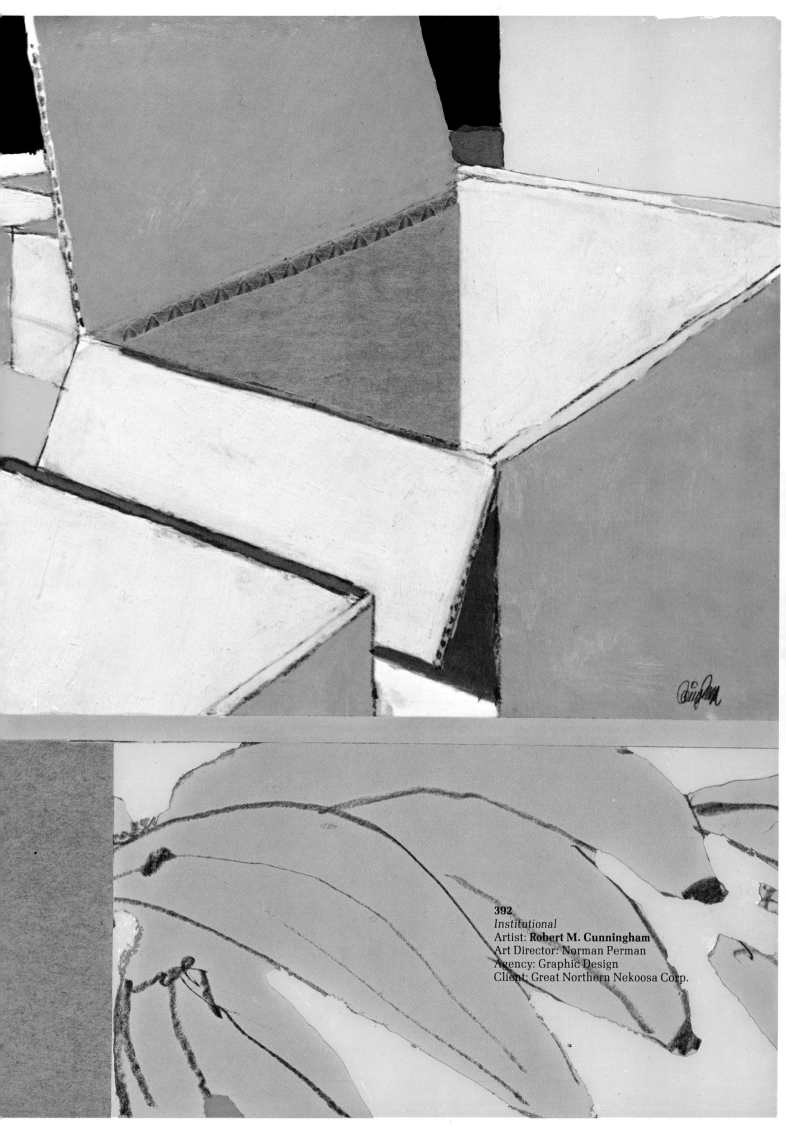

392
Institutional
Artist: **Robert M. Cunningham**
Art Director: Norman Perman
Agency: Graphic Design
Client: Great Northern Nekoosa Corp.

393
Book
Artist: **Betsy Roosen Sheppard**
Art Director: Betsy Roosen Sheppard

394
Advertising
Artist: **Charles Lilly**
Art Director: Jean Finley/Bob Gavin
Client: Caedmon Records

395
TV/Film
Artist: **Gerard Huerta**
Director: Bill Snyder/Herman Aronson
Producer: Jack Zander/Mark Zander
Production Company: Zander's Animation Parlour
Client: CBS Television Network
Award for Excellence

396
Book
Artist: **Marvin Simmons**
Art Director: Rick Benzel
Title: French for Communication II
Publisher: Houghton Mifflin Company

397
Editorial
Artist: **Debbie Kuhn**
Art Director: Joc Brooks
Publication: Penthouse Magazine

399
Institutional
Artist: **Jöseph Sumichrast**
Art Director: Connie Young
Agency: Foote, Cone, Belding & Honig, Inc.
Client: Levi Strauss & Co.

398
Advertising
Artist: **Jerry L. Cosgrove**
Art Director: B. Martin Pedersen
Agency: Jonson, Pedersen, Hinrichs & Shakery
Client: Martex Towels

400
Editorial
Artist: **Richard D. Harvey**
Art Director: Maxine Davidowitz
Publication: Redbook Magazine

401
Advertising
Artist: **Alan Magee**
Art Director: Alan Magee

402
Editorial
Artist: **Richard D. Harvey**
Art Director: Modesto Torre
Publication: McCall's Magazine

403
Book
Artist: **Nicholas Gaetano**
Art Director: Lynn Hollyn
Title: Walk Gently This Good Earth
Publisher: G.P. Putnam's Sons

As the final hour drew near, there was a buzzing of merriment and activity at the North Pole...

404
Institutional
Artist: **Gordon Kibbee**
Art Director: Gordon Kibbee

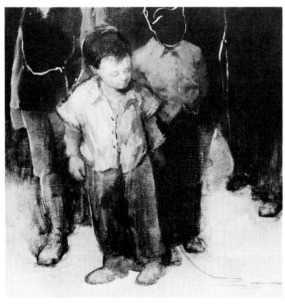
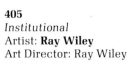

405
Institutional
Artist: **Ray Wiley**
Art Director: Ray Wiley

406
Book
Artist: **Raymond Briggs**
Art Director: Grace Clarke
Title: The Snowman
Publisher: Random House, Inc.

407
Institutional
Artist: **Robert Pepper**
Art Director: Geoffry Willsey
Client: Sunrise Cards

408
Advertising
Artist: **John C. Wallner**
Art Director: Christine Stawicki
Client: Children's Book Council

409
Editorial
Artist: **Marvin Mattelson**
Art Director: Carveth Kramer
Publication: Psychology Today

410
Book
Artist: **John M. Thompson**
Art Director: Barbara Bertoli
Title: The Summer of the Swans
Publisher: Avon Books

411
Institutional
Artist: **David P. Schulz**
Art Director: David P. Schulz
Client: Play Center Cooperative

412
Book
Artist: **Joanne Scribner**
Art Director: Bruce W. Hall
Title: Macaroon
Publisher: Dell Publishing Co., Inc.

413
Institutional
Artist: **Holly Hobbie**
Art Director: Ray Kowalski
Client: American Greetings Corp.

414
Institutional
Artist: **Holly Hobbie**
Art Director: Ray Kowalski
Client: American Greetings Corp.

415
Institutional
Artist: **Holly Hobbie**
Art Director: Ray Kowalski
Client: American Greetings Corp.

416
Advertising
Artist: **Mark English**
Art Director: Charles Walz
Client: Abbott Laboratories

417
Editorial
Artist: **Mark English**
Art Director: Bruce Danbrot/Don Adamec
Publication: Ladies' Home Journal

418
Editorial
Artist: **Daniel Schwartz**
Art Director: Nat Brandt
Publication: Publishers Weekly

419
Institutional
Artist: **B. J. Johnson**
Art Director: B. J. Johnson
Client: Ballet Metropolitan

420
Book
Artist: **Jerry Pinkney**
Art Director: Gordon Fisher
Title: Gulliver's Travels
Publisher: The Franklin Library

421
Book
Artist: **Lou Glanzman**
Art Director: Leonard Leone
Title: Kristin Lavransdatter III
Publisher: Bantam Books, Inc.

422
Institutional
Artist: **Sue Llewellyn**
Art Director: Sue Llewellyn
Client: Jack Strong
Award for Excellence

423
Book
Artist: **Errol Le Cain**
Art Director: Barbara Hennessy
Title: Twelve Dancing Princesses
Publisher: The Viking Press

424
Advertising
Artist: **Gordon Swenarton**
Art Director: Gordon Swenarton
Client: Aron & Falcone, Inc.

425
Editorial
Artist: **Jim Spanfeller**
Art Director: Marleen Adlerblum
Publication: Redbook Magazine

426
Editorial
Artist: **Skip Liepke**
Art Director: Skip Liepke

427
Book
Artist: **Barron Storey**
Art Director: Tom VonDerLinn
Title: The Great White Whale
Publisher: Reader's Digest

428
Book
Artist: **Barron Storey**
Art Director: Tom VonDerLinn
Title: The Great White Whale
Publisher: Reader's Digest

429
Book
Artist: **Barron Storey**
Art Director: Tom VonDerLinn
Title: The Great White Whale
Publisher: Reader's Digest

430
Book
Artist: **David Wenzel**
Art Director: Don Grant
Title: Middle Earth — The World of Tolkien
    Illustrated
Publisher: Centaur Books

431
Book
Artist: **Murray Tinkelman**
Art Director: Milton Charles
Title: Memed My Hawk
Publisher: Pocket Books

432
Book
Artist: **Murray Tinkelman**
Art Director: Milton Charles
Title: Eyes Etc.
Publisher: Pocket Books

433
Book
Artist: **David Palladini**
Art Director: Barbara Bertoli
Title: The Wife of Bath
Publisher: Avon Books

434
Advertising
Artist: **Bill Chambers**
Art Director: Bill Chambers

435
Institutional
Artist: **Mike Durbin**
Art Director: Mike Durbin

436
Institutional
Artist: **James McMullan**
Art Director: Carol Carson
Client: Scholastic Magazines, Inc.

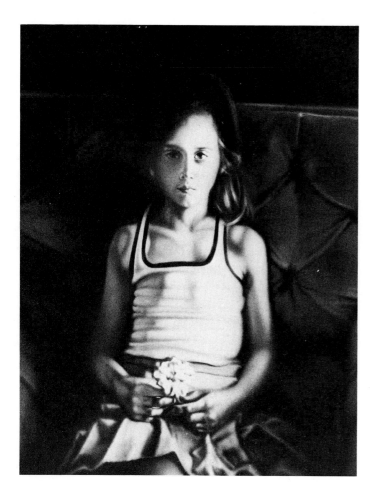

437
Book
Artist: **Jeanette Adams**
Art Director: Jeanette Adams

438
Institutional
Artist: **Reynold Ruffins**
Art Director: Diana Hrisinko
Client: Charles Scribner's Sons

439
Book
Artist: **Gahan Wilson**
Art Director: Lynn Hollyn
Title: "…and then we'll get him!"
Publisher: Richard Marek Publishers

440
Book
Artist: **Hank Virgona**
Art Director: Abe Lerner
Title: Rand Corporation
Publisher: Da Capo Press, Inc.

441
Book
Artist: **Chris Duke**
Art Director: Gordon Fisher
Title: Ibsen
Publisher: The Franklin Library

442
Book
Artist: **David Goodman Klein**
Art Director: David Goodman Klein

443
Editorial
Artist: **Gerry Gersten**
Art Director: Joe Connolly
Publication: Scouting Magazine

444
Book
Artist: **Rachel Isadora**
Art Director: Ava Weiss
Title: Back Stage
Publisher: Greenwillow Books

445
Book
Artist: **Reynold Ruffins**
Art Director: Diana Hrisinko
Title: Take Warning!
Publisher: Charles Scribner's Sons

446
Book
Artist: **Arnold Lobel**
Art Director: Ava Weiss
Title: Gregory Griggs
Publisher: Greenwillow Books

447
Book
Artist: **Brenda Pepper**
Art Director: Bruce W. Hall
Title: The Luck Book
Publisher: Dell Publishing Co., Inc.

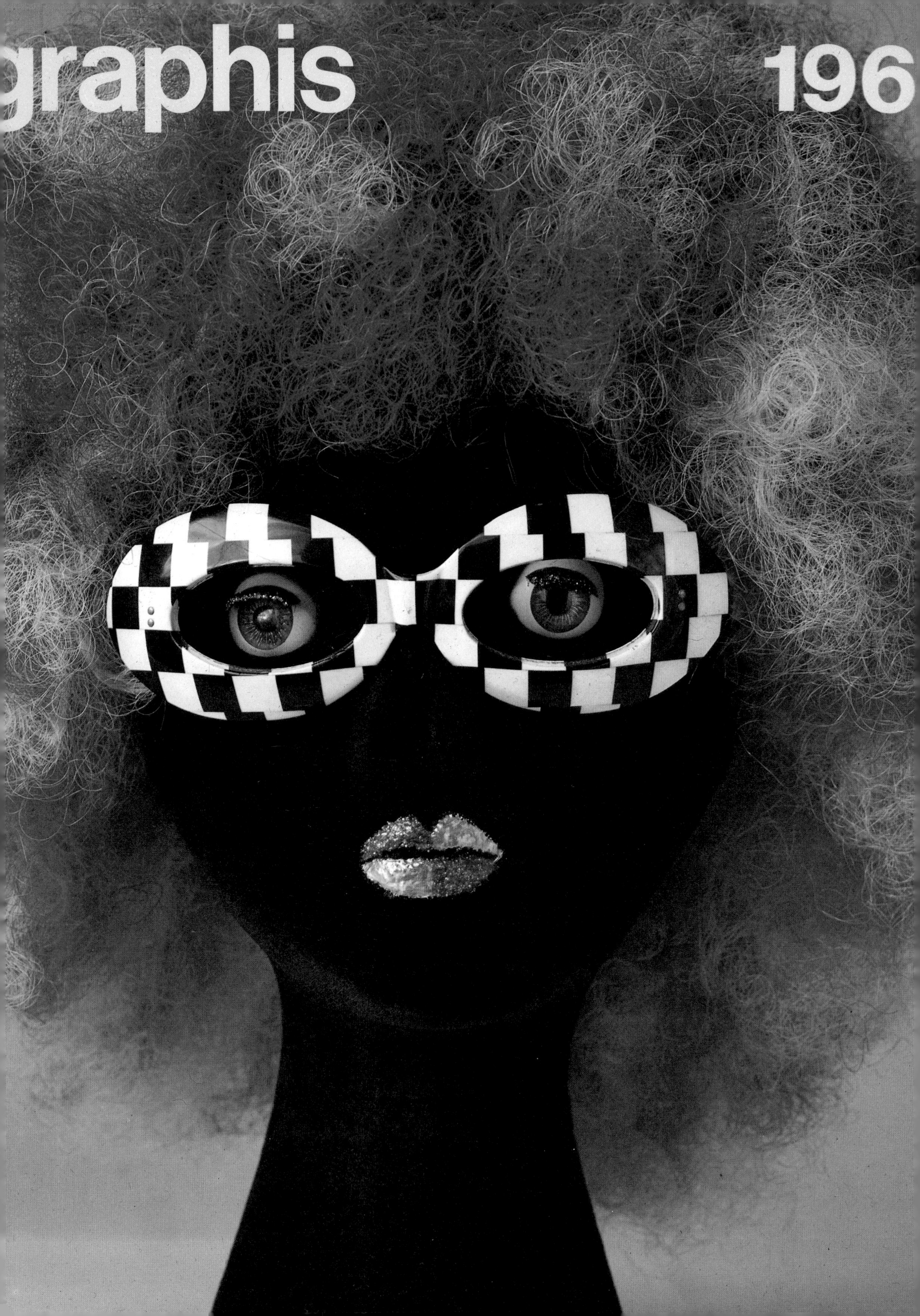
graphis
196

449
Institutional
Artist: **Leo & Diane Dillon**
Art Director: Leo & Diane Dillon
Client: Cathcart Gallery

450
Institutional
Artist: **Alvin J. Pimsler**
Art Director: Alvin J. Pimsler

448
Editorial
Artist: **Jacqui Morgan**
Art Director: Walter Herdeg
Publication: Graphis Magazine

451
Book
Artist: **John Collier**
Art Director: Janet Townsend
Title: Growing Up Guilty
Publisher: Pantheon Books
Gold Medal

452
Editorial
Artist: **Bart Forbes**
Art Director: Modesto Torre
Publication: McCall's Magazine

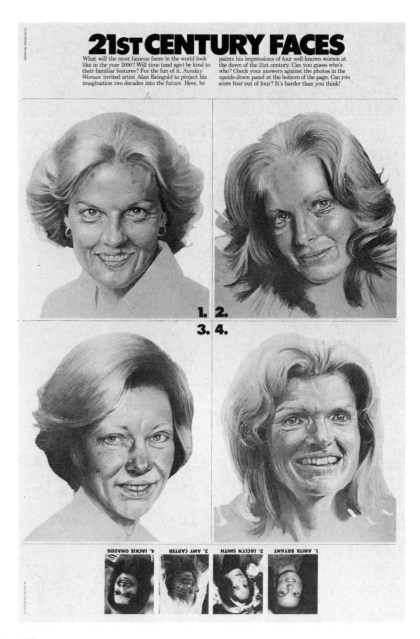

21ST CENTURY FACES

What will the most famous faces in the world look like in the year 2000? Will time (and age) be kind to their familiar features? For the fun of it, *Sunday Woman* invited artist Alan Reingold to project his imagination two decades into the future. Here, he paints his impressions of four well-known women at the dawn of the 21st century. Can you guess who's who? Check your answers against the photos in the upside-down panel at the bottom of the page. Can you score four out of four? It's harder than you think!

1. 2.
3. 4.

1. ANITA BRYANT 2. JACLYN SMITH 3. AMY CARTER 4. JACKIE ONASSIS

453
Editorial
Artist: **Alan Reingold**
Art Director: Estelle Walpin
Publication: Sunday Woman

454
TV/Still
Artist: **Kim Kolinski**
Art Director: Joe Sparkman
Client: WLS-TV

455
Advertising
Artist: **Wayne Salo**
Art Director: Wayne Salo
Agency: Diener, Hauser, Bates Co., Inc.
Client: Atlantic Releasing

456
Editorial
Artist: **Dennis Luzak**
Art Director: Al Grossman/Modesto Torre
Publication: McCall's Magazine

457
Book
Artist: **Richard Sparks**
Art Director: Lynn Hollyn
Title: The Wardens
Publisher: Richard Marek Publishers
Award for Excellence

458
Editorial
Artist: **Bob Peak**
Art Director: Bob Peak
Award for Excellence

Gertrude Stein and Her Fords

by Donald Hall

459
Editorial
Artist: **Max Altekruse**
Art Director: Malcom T. Young
Publication: Ford Times—Ford Motor Co.

460
Book
Artist: **Edward W. Acuña**
Art Director: Richard Carter
Publisher: Easton Press

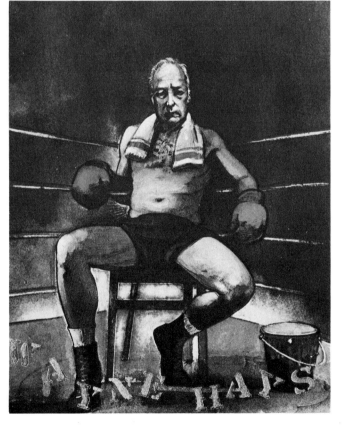

461
Editorial
Artist: **Daniel Maffia**
Art Director: Greg Paul
Publication: Ohio Magazine

462
Editorial
Artist: **Barron Storey**
Art Director: Bud Loader
Publication: Flying Magazine

463
Advertising
Artist: **Chet Jezierski**
Art Director: Stan Sweeney
Agency: W. B. Doner & Co.
Client: The National Guard

464
Editorial
Artist: **Elias Rivera**
Art Director: Carveth Kramer
Publication: Psychology Today

465
Institutional
Artist: **Fred Otnes**
Art Director: Fred Otnes
Agency: The Illustrators Workshop
Client: The New York Public Library

466
Institutional
Artist: **Fred Otnes**
Art Director: Fred Otnes
Agency: Master Eagle Gallery
Client: The Illustrators Workshop

467
Institutional
Artist: **Michael Ng**
Art Director: Michael Ng

468
Institutional
Artist: **Gary Kelley**
Art Director: Gary Kelley
Client: Hellman Design Associates

469
Book
Artist: **Mel Greifinger**
Art Director: Mel Greifinger

470
Editorial
Artist: **Fred Otnes**
Art Director: Joseph Connolly
Publication: Boys' Life Magazine

471
Editorial
Artist: **James Endicott**
Art Director: Tamara Schneider
Publication: Seventeen Magazine

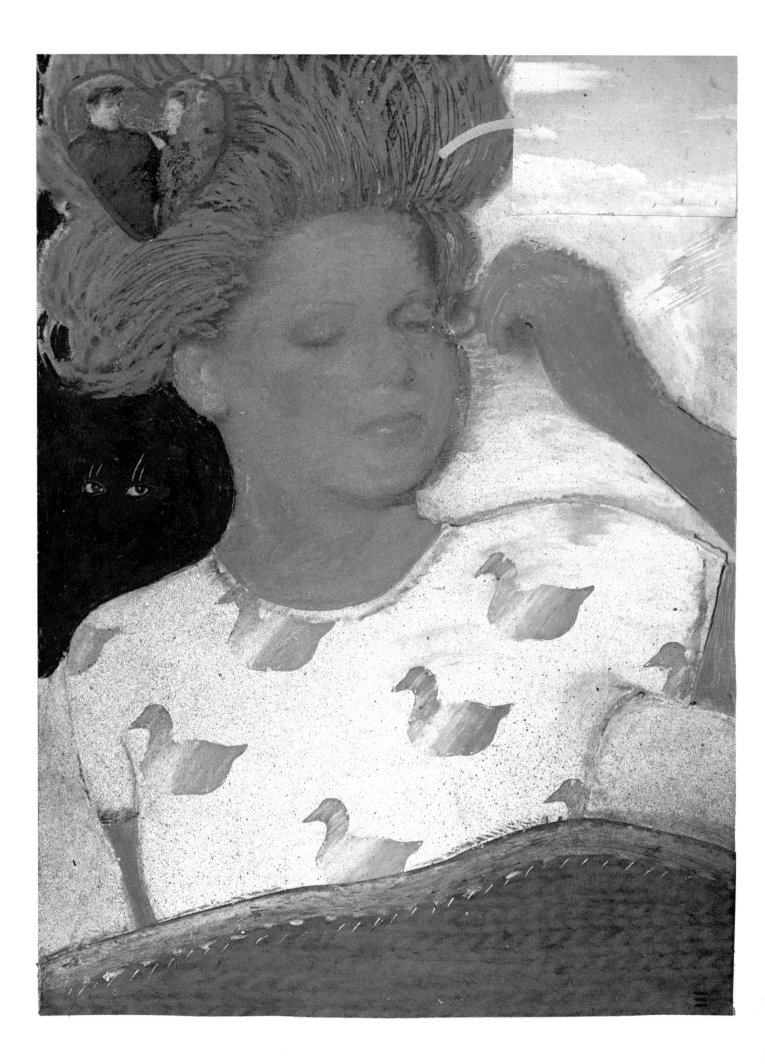

MOTHER
TO
DAUGHTER

473
Editorial
Artist: **George Angelini**
Art Director: Herb Bleiweiss
Publication: Good Housekeeping

474
Editorial
Artist: **Ellen Griesedieck**
Art Director: Noel Werrett
Publication: Quest Magazine

72
ditorial
rtist: **Eric Barnes**
rt Director: Dale Moyer/Mary Zisk
ublication: Action Magazine

475
Editorial
Artist: **Charles Santore**
Art Director: Jerry Alten
Publication: TV Guide

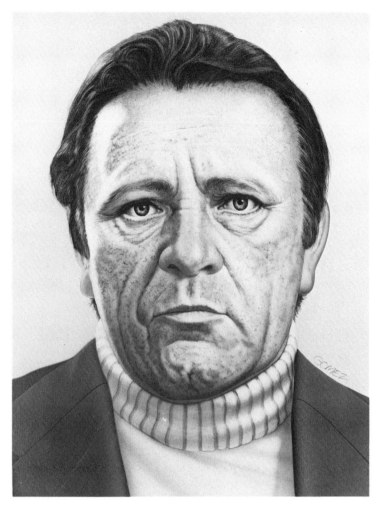

476
Editorial
Artist: **Ignacio Gomez**
Art Director: Michael Brock
Publication: Oui Magazine

477
Editorial
Artist: **Herb Davidson**
Art Director: Arthur Paul
Publication: Playboy Magazine

478
Advertising
Artist: **Peter M. Fiore**
Art Director: Peter M. Fiore
Award for Excellence

479
Advertising
Artist: **Bob Crofut**
Art Director: Bob Crofut

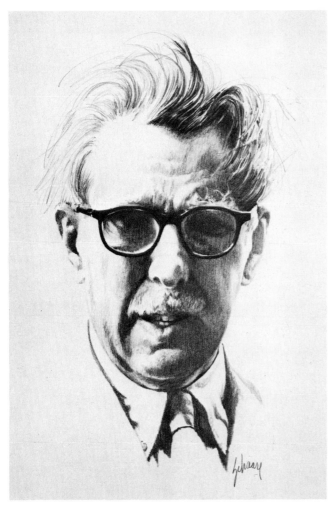

480
Book
Artist: **Harry J. Schaare**
Art Director: Harry J. Schaare
Title: Thurber
Publisher: The Franklin Library

481
Advertising
Artist: **Gerry Gersten**
Art Director: Dick Thomas
Agency: Lord, Geller, Federico, Einstein, Inc.
Client: Quality Paperbacks

482
Book
Artist: **Rick McCollum**
Art Director: William R. Gregory
Title: Doctor Crippen's Diary
Publisher: Reader's Digest

483
Editorial
Artist: **Richard L. Waldrep**
Art Director: Robert Barkin
Publication: Washington Post Magazine

484
TV/Still
Artist: **Kathleen Gray Farthing**
Art Director: James Denney, Jr.
Client: WTAE-TV News

485
Institutional
Artist: **Bob Lapsley**
Art Director: Bob Lapsley

486
Institutional
Artist: **Dick Lubey**
Art Director: Dick Lubey

487
Institutional
Artist: **James Barkley**
Art Director: Tom Haynes/Marc Rubin
Agency: Sudler & Hennessey, Inc.
Client: Stuart Pharmaceuticals

488
Editorial
Artist: **Roy Andersen**
Art Director: Walter Bernard
Publication: Time Magazine

489
Editorial
Artist: **Burt Silverman**
Art Director: Walter Bernard
Publication: Time Magazine

490
Editorial
Artist: **Gerry Gersten**
Art Director: Irene Ramp/Walter Bernard
Publication: Time Magazine

491
Editorial
Artist: **Alex Gnidziejko**
Art Director: Joe Brooks
Publication: Penthouse Magazine

492
Editorial
Artist: **Alex Gnidziejko**
Art Director: Joe Brooks
Publication: Penthouse Magazine

494
Book
Artist: **Rich Cooper**
Art Director: Rich Cooper

493
Advertising
Artist: **Alvin J. Pimsler**
Art Director: Alvin J. Pimsler

495
Editorial
Artist: **Daniel Schwartz**
Art Director: Ron Campbell
Publication: Fortune Magazine

496
Editorial
Artist: **Steve Karchin**
Art Director: Alice Degenhardt
Publication: Creative Living Magazine

497
Editorial
Artist: **Wilson McLean**
Art Director: Joe Brooks
Publication: Penthouse Magazine

499
Book
Artist: **Sandy Kossin**
Art Director: Leonard Leone
Title: The American Way of Laughing
Publisher: Bantam Books, Inc.

498
Advertising
Artist: **Walt Spitzmiller**
Art Director: Dolores Gudzin
Client: NBC Television

500
Advertising
Artist: **David Levine**
Art Director: Henrietta Condak
Client: CBS Records

The Assassination of Martin

501
Editorial
Artist: **Alan E. Cober**
Art Director: Gordon Mortensen
Publication: Politics Today Magazine

502
Editorial
Artist: **Burt Silverman**
Art Director: Irving Miller/M. Glaubach
Publication: 1199 News Magazine
National Union of Hospital &
Health Care Employees—AFL-CIO

503
Editorial
Artist: **Richard Sparks**
Art Director: Joseph Connolly
Publication: Scouting Magazine

504
Editorial
Artist: **Jean Mulatier**
Art Director: Walter Bernard
Publication: Time Magazine

CARTERGATE V

THE FIRST HUNDRED LIES OF JIMMY CARTER

When he was running for office, our president
told us that he would never, never tell a lie. On the contrary,
it is extremely difficult for him to tell the truth.

BY CRAIG S. KARPEL

Jimmy Carter is a liar.
The president of the United States is a habitual, compulsive teller of untruths
who, throughout his campaign and administration, has woven a tangled web of
false and misleading statements.

53

505
Editorial
Artist: **Steve Pietzsch**
Art Director: Joe Brooks
Publication: Penthouse

506
Institutional
Artist: **Reed Merrill**
Art Director: Reed Merrill

507
Book
Artist: **Edward Sorel**
Art Director: Ken Miyamoto
Title: Make Believe Presidents
Publisher: Pantheon Books, Inc.

CAROL WALD

509
Advertising
Artist: **Cyril David**
Art Director: Cyril David

510
Advertising
Artist: **Cyril David**
Art Director: Cyril David

508
Editorial
Artist: **Carol Wald**
Art Director: Jessica M. Weber
Publication: International Review of
            Food & Wine

511
Institutional
Artist: **Tom McNeely**
Art Director: Gary Greer
Agency: Unicover Corporation
Client: Fleetwood

512
Institutional
Artist: **Tom McNeely**
Art Director: Gary Greer
Client: Fleetwood

INTERNATIONAL SECTION

The Society's scope of influence in exposing the talents of commercial artists to an ever-widening audience has resulted in an increasing demand for our Annual Show and Exhibition to include more representation from markets outside our own country.

In answer to these demands the first foreign section was added last year to Illustrators 20. Its immediate success was evident by this year's avalanche of entries from many of the world's markets. We are anticipating that this section will continue to expand for years to come.

513
Institutional
Artist: **Masazumi Fujita**
Art Director: Masazumi Fujita
Agency: The Atelier Co., Ltd.
Client: Canadian Enterprises, Inc.

出かけるか。明日へ

おかげさまで1周年。
SEIBU
西武
春日井
ショッピングセンター
19号線バイパス沿い

514
Advertising
Artist: **Shigeo Okamoto**
Art Director: Shigeo Okamoto
Agency: Shigeo Okamoto Design Center
Client: Seibu Kasugai Shopping Center
Award for Excellence

515
Advertising
Artist: **Shigeo Okamoto**
Art Director: Shigeo Okamoto
Agency: Shigeo Okamoto Design Center
Client: Meitetsu Sakae Melsa

516
Advertising
Artist: **Shigeo Okamoto**
Art Director: Shigeo Okamoto

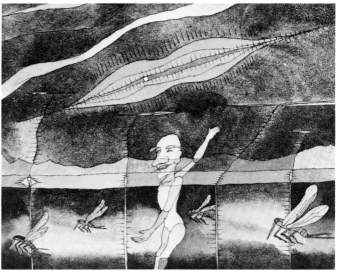

517
Advertising
Artist: **Hidenobu Ito**
Art Director: Hidenobu Ito
Client: Gallery Seki

518
Advertising
Artist: **Hidenobu Ito**
Art Director: Hidenobu Ito
Client: Gallery Anri

519
Advertising
Artist: **Masaru Suzuki**
Art Director: Masaru Suzuki

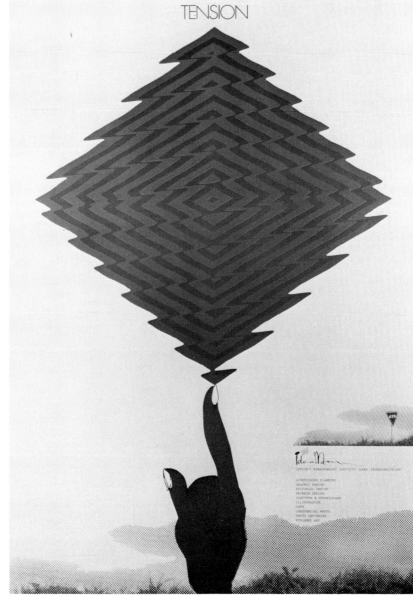

520
Advertising
Artist: **Katsuyuki Sumi**
Art Director: Katsuyuki Sumi

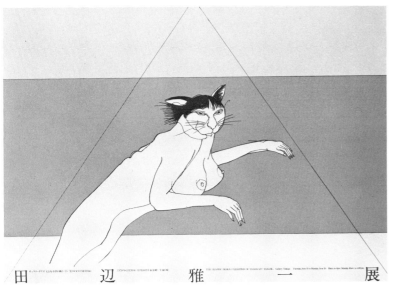

521
Advertising
Artist: **Masakazu Tanabe**
Art Director: Masakazu Tanabe
Client: Gallery Takega

522
Editorial
Artist: **Gordon Halloran**
Art Director: Robert Priest
Publication: Weekend Magazine

523
Editorial
Artist: **Ryu-Kumita**
Art Director: Ryu-Kumita
Publication:
Award for Excellence

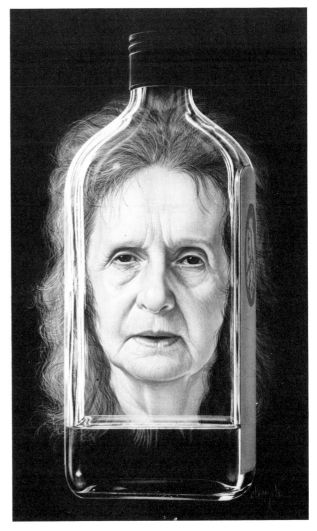

524
Editorial
Artist: **Eraldo Carugati**
Art Director: Robert Priest
Publication: Weekend Magazine

525
Institutional
Artist: **Michael McKeever**
Art Director: Michael McKeever
Client: Manufacturers Life Insurance Co.

526
Editorial
Artist: **Tom McNeely**
Art Director: John Strimas
Publication: Business Journal

527
Advertising
Artist: **Pat Michener**
Art Director: Pat Michener

528
Advertising
Artist: **Pat Michener**
Art Director: Pat Michener
Award for Excellence

529
Advertising
Artist: **Nobuyuki Nishihara**
Art Director: Nobuyuki Nishihara

530
Editorial
Artist: **Gabriel Pascalini**
Art Director: Robert Priest
Publication: Weekend Magazine

531
Advertising
Artist: **Masazumi Fujita**
Art Director: Masazumi Fujita
Client: The Atelier Co., Ltd.

532
Advertising
Artist: **Yukiko Goto**
Art Director: Yukiko Goto

533
Advertising
Artist: **Noriko Otobe**
Art Director: Noriko Otobe

534
Advertising
Artist: **Yoshie Tanaka**
Art Director: Yoshie Tanaka

535
Advertising
Artist: **Ted Michener**
Art Director: Ted Michener

536
Editorial
Artist: **Katsuhiko Ikeda**
Art Director: Katsuhiko Ikeda
Publication: Sanrio Co., Ltd.

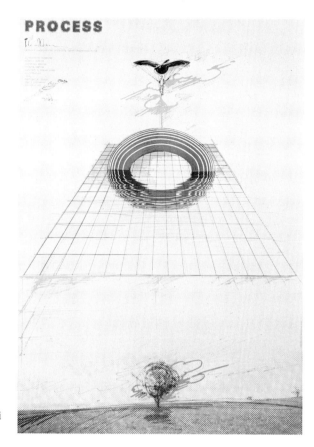

PROCESS

537
Advertising
Artist: **Katsuyuki Sumi**
Art Director: Katsuyuki Sumi
Agency: Idea-Man

538
Book
Artist: **Carol Lawson**
Art Director: Ivan Tyrrell
Title: Childe Roland
Publisher: Harcourt Brace Jovanovich, Inc.

539
Advertising
Artist: **Keiji Sugita**
Art Director: Keiji Sugita
Client: Keiji Sugita Design Office

540
Advertising
Artist: **Yukihisa Takakita**
Art Director: Yukihisa Takakita
Client: Hakuzen Gallery

明日がみえるかな。

541
Advertising
Artist: **Shigeo Okamoto**
Art Director: Shigeo Okamoto
Client: Seibu Kasugai Shopping Center

542
Book
Artist: **John Butler**
Art Director: Bernard Higton
Title: Street Pigeon
Publisher: Hutchinsons Ltd., Publishers

543
Advertising
Artist: **Shuzo Kato**
Art Director: Shuzo Kato

544
Advertising
Artist: **Yoshikatsu Kosakai**
Art Director: Yoshikatsu Kosakai
Agency: Ad-Brain Center
Client: Nagaragawa Hotel

545
Advertising
Artist: **Shuzo Kato**
Art Director: Shuzo Kato

546
Book
Artist: **Ann Meisel**
Art Director: Ann Meisel
Title: Duke Ellington
Publisher: Sphere Books

547
Institutional
Artist: **Yoshikazu Nakata**
Art Director: Yoshikazu Nakata

548
Book
Artist: **Adrian Day**
Art Director: Adrian Day

549
Editorial
Artist: **Michael McKeever**
Art Director: Michael McKeever

550
Advertising
Artist: **Ann Meisel**
Art Director: Graham Cornthwaite
Agency: Cherry, Hedger, Seymour
Client: Royal Pie Fillings

551
Advertising
Artist: **Pat Michener**
Art Director: Pat Michener
Client: Sullivan Studios

552
Editorial
Artist: **Heather Cooper**
Art Director: Robert Priest
Publication: Weekend Magazine

553
Advertising
Artist: **Pat Michener**
Art Director: Pat Michener

554
Editorial
Artist: **Julian Allen**
Art Director: Jean De Machy
Publication: French Playboy Magazine

555
Editorial
Artist: **Fluck/Law**
Art Director: Robert Priest
Publication: Weekend Magazine

556
Editorial
Artist: **Maurice Kennel**
Art Director: Dick De Moeï
Publication: Avenue

557
Book
Artist: **Les Edwards**
Art Director: Dom Rodi
Title: Thongor Fights the Pirates of Tarakus
Publisher: Star Books

558
Book
Artist: **Jim Burns**
Art Director: Philip Dunn
Title: Colonel Kylling
Publisher: Pierrot Publishing

560
Editorial
Artist: **Ralph Steadman**
Art Director: Robert Priest
Publication: Weekend Magazine

559
Editorial
Artist: **Maurice Kennel**
Art Director: Dick De Moeï
Publication: Avenue

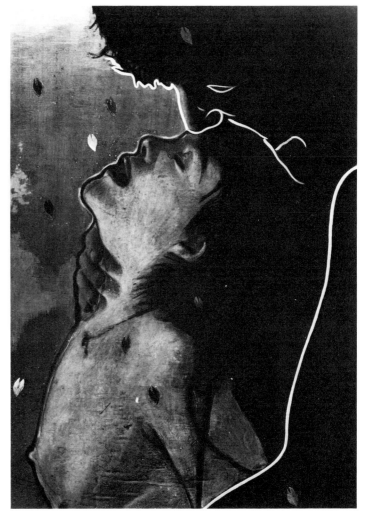

561
Editorial
Artist: **Toshio Komada**
Art Director: Toshio Komada
Publication: City Union

562
Editorial
Artist: **Toshio Komada**
Art Director: Toshio Komada
Publication: City Union

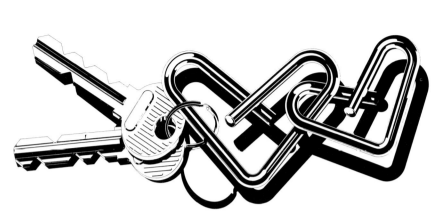

563
Editorial
Artist: **Syunyo Yamauchi**
Art Director: Syunyo Yamauchi

564
Editorial
Artist: **Syunyo Yamauchi**
Art Director: Syunyo Yamauchi

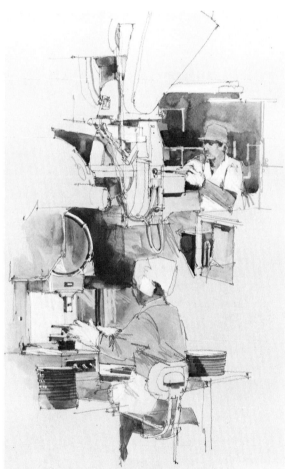

565
Advertising
Artist: **Masazumi Fujita**
Art Director: Masazumi Fujita
Agency: The Atelier Co., Ltd.
Client: Tayoshi Sangyo Co., Ltd.

566
Editorial
Artist: **Yoshikazu Nakata**
Art Director: Toshihisa Nishio
Publication: Kanefusa Knife & Saw Co., Ltd.
Annual Report

567
Book
Artist: **Jim Burns**
Art Director: Philip Dunn
Title: Mechanismo 1
Publisher: Pierrot Publishing

568
Book
Artist: **Jim Burns**
Art Director: Philip Dunn
Title: Mechanismo 2
Publisher: Pierrot Publishing

THE 3rd EXHIBITION OF GRAPHIC DESIGNERS CLUB

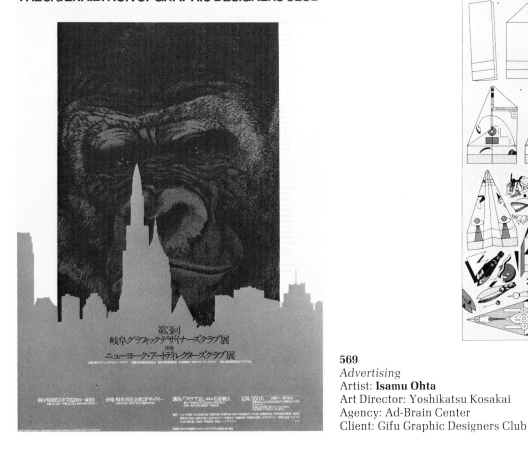

569
Advertising
Artist: **Isamu Ohta**
Art Director: Yoshikatsu Kosakai
Agency: Ad-Brain Center
Client: Gifu Graphic Designers Club

570
Institutional
Artist: **Chris McEwan**
Art Director: Chris McEwan

571
Institutional
Artist: **Sadahito Mori**
Art Director: Sadahito Mori

572
Advertising
Artist: **Sadahito Mori**
Art Director: Sadahito Mori
Client: Sentimental City Romance

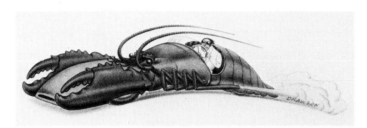

573
Editorial
Artist: **Blair Drawson**
Art Director: Robert Priest
Publication: Weekend Magazine

574
Institutional
Artist: **Sadahito Mori**
Art Director: Sadahito Mori
Client: Illustrators Nagoya

575
Editorial
Artist: **Isamu Ohta**
Art Director: Isamu Ohta
Publication: The Shingfu Department
Stores Ltd.

576
Editorial
Artist: **Peter Swan**
Art Director: Robert Priest
Publication: Weekend Magazine

577
Editorial
Artist: **Katsuhiko Ikeda**
Art Director: Katsuhiko Ikeda
Publication: Sanrio Co., Ltd.

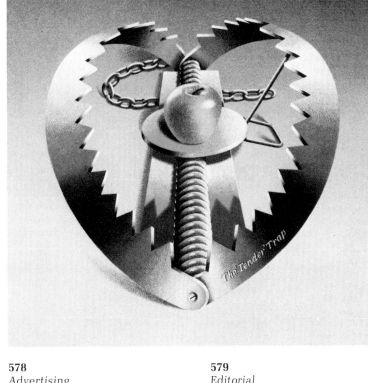

578
Advertising
Artist: **Masakazu Tanabe**
Art Director: Masakazu Tanabe
Client: Gallery Takega

579
Editorial
Artist: **Peter Brookes**
Art Director: Robert Priest
Publication: Weekend Magazine

580
Advertising
Artist: **Masakazu Tanabe**
Art Director: Masakazu Tanabe
Client: Gallery Takega

581
Editorial
Artist: **Alex Murawski**
Art Director: Robert Priest/Derek Ungless
Publication: Weekend Magazine

582
Advertising
Artist: **Toshikane Tanaka**
Art Director: Toshikane Tanaka

583
Editorial
Artist: **Peter Till**
Art Director: Robert Priest
Publication: Weekend Magazine

584
Editorial
Artist: **A. Leimanis**
Art Director: Steward Gray
Publication: The Montreal Star

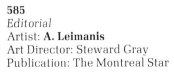

585
Editorial
Artist: **A. Leimanis**
Art Director: Steward Gray
Publication: The Montreal Star

586
Editorial
Artist: **A. Leimanis**
Art Director: Steward Gray
Publication: The Montreal Star

ILLUSTRATORS 21 Index

While the Society of Illustrators and Hastings House make every effort possible to publish full and correct credits for each work included in this volume, sometimes errors of omission or commission do creep in. For these, the Society and Hastings House are most regretful, but hereby must disclaim any liability other than their promise to the aggrieved party to do better next time.

As this book is printed in process colors, we regret that the original colors of some of the illustrations reproduced here have been altered.

ILLUSTRATORS

Adams, Jeanette, 437
247 East 77 Street
New York City

Acuña, Edward W., 460
48 Dawn Street
Fairfield, CT

Alcorn, John, 52, 110, 118,
119, 327
35 Paulding Avenue
Cold Springs, NY

Allen, Julian, 224, 320, 554
31 Walker Street
New York City

Allen, Thomas B., 346
P.O. Box 1919
Sag Harbor, NY

Altekruse, Max, 459
26025 Carol
Franklin, MI

Ameijide, Ray, 109, 126, 127, 174
251 East 51 Street
New York City

Andersen, Roy, 176, 488
121 St. John's Road
Ridgefield, CT

Angelini, George, 473
4 Churchill Street
Ossining, NY

Arisman, Marshall, 54
314 West 100th Street
New York City

Barkley, James, 487
25 Brook Manor
Pleasantville, NY

Barnes, Eric, 472
255 West 85 Street
New York City

Barr, Diane, 63
22501 Mylls
St. Clair Shores, MI

Beckhardt, Karen, 135
322 West 106 Street
New York City

Bellerose, Mark, 231
275 Newbury Street
Boston, MA

Berge, James Franklin, 225
191 Lexington Avenue
Westwood, NJ

Berkey, John, 9, 220, 222,
251, 252
c/o Frank & Jeff Lavaty
45 East 51 Street
New York City

Berman, Steve, 101
9343 Oak Park Avenue
Morton Grove, IL

Bond, Barbara Higgins, 380
304 Woodbine
Teaneck, NJ

Brautigam, Don, 59
29 Cona Court
Haledon, NJ

Brewer, Bill, 158
Hallmark Cards
25th & McGee
Kansas City, MO

Brickner, Alice, 92
4720 Grosvenor Avenue
Bronx, NY

Briggs, Raymond, 406
c/o Julia MacRae
Hamish Hamilton Children's
Books, Ltd.
Garden House
557-9 Long Acre
London, WC2, England

Brody, Marion, 193
640 West Roscoe
Chicago, IL

Brookes, Peter, 579
30 Vanbrugh Hill
London, England
SE3 7UF

Brown, Harry, 159
c/o Hallmark Cards
25th & McGee
Kansas City, MO

Brown, Michael David, 123,
202, 243
416 Hungerford Drive
Rockville, MD

Bru, Salvador, 5
7910 Woodmond Avenue #1104
Bethesda, MD

Brunner-Strosser, Ruth, 212
1033 Grandview Avenue
Pittsburgh, PA

Burns, Jim, 67, 558, 567, 568
c/o Philip Dunn Agency
Pierrot Publishing Ltd.
17 Oakley Road
London, N1-3LL, England

Butcher, Jim, 269
c/o Frank & Jeff Lavaty
45 East 51 Street
New York City

Butler, John, 542
3 Carlisle Street
London, England
W1

Byrd, David, 39
17 West 17th Street
New York City

Campbell, Alice, 138
4848 Guiton, Suite 222
Houston, TX

Carugati, Eraldo, 46, 524
1567 Ridge
Evanston, IL

Catalano, Sal, 82, 378
114 Boyce Place
Ridgewood, NJ

Chambers, Bill, 129, 434
1607 S. Harvard
Arlington Heights, IL

Chase, Ben, 53
520 East Sixth Street
New York City

Christensen, James C., 167
656 West 550 South
Oren, UT

Chwast, Seymour, 355
Pushpin Studio
207 East 32 Street
New York City

Ciardiello, Joe, 230
203 Center Street
Staten Island, NY

Ciccarelli, Gary, 324
25334 Rouge River Drive
Dearborn Heights, MI

Cober, Alan E., 2, 3, 40, 156, 501
Croton Dam Road
Ossining, NY

CoConis, Ted, 8, 10, 157
2140 Bush Street
San Francisco, CA

Colby, Garry, 85
McNamara Association
2350 Penobscot Building
Detroit, MI

Collier, John, 6, 78, 266, 293,
331, 451
North Quaker Hill Road
Pawling, NY

Colonna, Bernard, 221
c/o C. Bancroft
185 Goodhill Road
Weston, CT

Conahan, Jim, 173
520 N. Michigan
Chicago, IL

Condak, Cliff, 284, 333
Moffett Road
Cold Spring, NY

Cooper, Heather, 552
Burns/Cooper/Hynes
96 Bloor Street West
Toronto, Ontario

Cooper, Rich, 494
247 Hastings, NE
Grand Rapids, MI

Cosgrove, Jerry L., 398
223 East 31 Street
New York City

Cox, Peter, 66
National Arts Club
15 Gramercy Park
New York City

Craft, Kinuko, 164
1940 North Hudson
Chicago, IL

Crist, Richard, 112
58 Glasco Turnpike
Woodstock, NY

ART DIRECTORS

FILM DIRECTORS

FILM PRODUCERS

FILM PRODUCTION

see under AGENCIES

CLIENTS

PUBLISHERS

AGENCIES

TITLES

ILLUSTRATORS 21 Production Credits

The type in this book is
Melior with Helvetica

Composition by
M.J. Baumwell, Typography

Offset plates and printing by
Connecticut Printers, Inc.

The paper is
Midtech Optimum Dull

Paper Supplier
Andrews/Nelson/Whitehead Publishing Papers

Binding by
A. Horowitz and Son

Jacket printed by
Princeton Polychrome Press

Production supervision
James Moore, Hastings House

ADVERTISERS
Artists Associates
Gordon Associates Ltd., Barbara
Hankins, David
Illustrators Workshop, The
Independent Study Degree Programs
    of Syracuse University
Jarvis, David
Kirchoff/Wohlberg, Inc.
Kursár, Raymond

Little Darling's

KRISTY MC NICKOL
TATUM O'NEAL

THE BRADFORD BOOK OF
COLLECTOR'S PLATES

SCARLETT

*First issue in the Gone with the Wind Collection,
based on the immortal movie.*

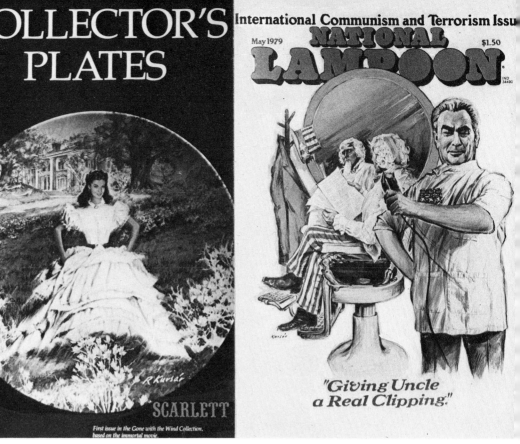

International Communism and Terrorism Issu

May 1979   NATIONAL LAMPOON $1.50

*"Giving Uncle
a Real Clipping."*

Realistic art and art styles Imitated by
artist: Raymond Kursár

One Lincoln Plaza-New York, N.Y. 10023
To view Portfolio call (212) 873-5605

See other ads in Illustrators Annuals, 15, 18, 19, 20

KING of HEARTS
a new musical

ADAMS
DENTYNE
CHEWING GUM
HELPS KEEP TEETH WHITE

Helps keep teeth white, breath fresh.

GERALDINE PAGE   KENNETH HAIGH

*Tennessee Williams'
Clothes for a
Summer Hotel*

Scenic Production Designed by
OLIVER SMITH
Costumes by
THEONI V. ALDREDGE
Lighting by
MARILYN RENNAGEL
Directed by
JOSÉ QUINTERO

artists

Norman Adams, Robert Heindel,
Steve Karchin, Dick Krepel,
Norman LaLiberte, Dennis Luzak,
Rick McCollum, Fred Otnes.

Represented by:
Bill Erlacher, Artists Associates
211 East 51 Street, New York, N.Y. 10022
Telephone: (212) 755-1365/6
Associates: Eileen McMahon,
Madeline Renard

It Takes Masters To Make Masters...

*PAUL DAVIS
ROBERT GROSSMAN
RICHARD HARVEY
DOUG JOHNSON
MARVIN MATTLESON
JAMES McMULLEN
JACQUI MORGAN
REYNOLD RUFFINS
LEE SAVAGE
ISADORE SELTZER
MURRAY TINKELMAN
ROBERT WEAVER

*Some of the greatest names in Illustration, what else do they have in common? They have all been summer faculty in Syracuse University's Independent Study Master of Fine Arts in Illustration program.

The Syracuse program is designed for the professional who wants to continue working full time and yet improve his skills and earn a degree in a relatively short period. The program is intensive, you'll be challenged, moved out of your rut, and you'll grow, grow, grow. If you'd like to spend a few weeks a year working with some of the top professionals while earning an MFA degree:

call or write
Syracuse University,
(315)-423-3269

Independent Study Degree Programs
Rm 302 Reid Hall, 610 East Fayette St.,
Syracuse, N.Y., 13202

OUR TEN COMMANDMENTS of ARTIST REPRESENTATION

1. We represent only artists we believe in and are totally committed to them.

2. We believe in being more than agents and become involved in the *total career* of the artists we represent.

3. We appreciate the problems of the artist and try, whenever possible, to alleviate these problems.

4. We also appreciate the problems of the art director: his client-agency relationship, tight deadlines and budget limitations and try to help him solve these problems whenever we can.

5. We believe in *full representation*. That means taking on only that number of artists that we can fully represent as well as insuring that each artist is non-competitive in style with other artists we represent.

6. We believe in giving *full service* to our artists and to the art director, promptly and professionally. Every client, no matter what the job price, deserves the very best we can offer.

7. We believe in being *flexible*. Business conditions change. The economy rises and falls. Accounts switch. We and our artists must adjust to all changes in order to successfully survive.

8. We believe in always meeting deadlines and always keeping a bargain. We and our artists are only as good as our word and our last job.

9. We believe in *BEING HONEST* at all times. With our artists. With the art director. With ourselves.

10. And finally, we believe in our *profession* . . . the profession of representing artists. We firmly believe that it is the most exciting and challenging profession anywhere and we are proud to be a part of it.

Barbara & Elliott Gordon

**Barbara Gordon
Associates Ltd.
165 East 32 Street
New York, N.Y. 10016
212-686-3514**

FOR INFORMATION ON BARBARA GORDON PUBLICATIONS AVAILABLE,
WRITE TO US AT THE ABOVE ADDRESS.

KIRCHOFF/WOHLBERG

Angela Adams
Bob Barner
Marc Brown
Brian Cody
Helen Cogancherry
Beatrice Darwin
Arlene Dubanevich
Alex Ebel
Lois Ehlert
Frank Fretz
Rosalind Fry
Jon Goodell
Konrad Hack
Michael Hampshire
Hilary Hayton
Ronald Himler
Rosekrans Hoffman
Gerry Hoover
Fred Irvin
Frances Jetter
Harvey Kidder
Daniel Kirk
Dora Leder
Ronald LeHew
Susan Lexa
Don Madden
Stefan Martin
Carolyn McHenry
Erica Merkling
Lyle Miller
Carol Nicklaus
Ed Parker
Susan Perl
Charles Robinson
Joseph A. Smith
Douglas Snow
Arvis Stewart
Phero Thomas
Helen Tullen
Lou Vaccaro
Alexandra Wallner
John Wallner

KIRCHOFF/WOHLBERG, INC.
ARTISTS REPRESENTATIVE

433 EAST 51 ST., NEW YORK, N.Y. 10022
212-753-5146
897 BOSTON POST RD., MADISON, CT. 06443
203-245-7308

David Hankins

Represents:

GREG KING

WALTER RANE

DAVID JARVIS

HARRY SCHAARE

JOE ISOM

MARIO STASOLLA

Advertising and Editorial Art   **Call** (212) 867-8092

Paramount Pictures Presents A Lawrence Gordon Production "THE WARRIORS"
Art Director Ed Brodkin   Designer Ed Harridsleff   Agency Diener Hauser Bates
Illustrator David Jarvis   Represented by David Hankins PhD   (212) 867-8092

R RESTRICTED
UNDER 17 REQUIRES ACCOMPANYING
PARENT OR ADULT GUARDIAN

Directed by Walter Hill   Read the Dell Book

THE ILLUSTRATORS WORKSHOP

Alan E. Cober, Mark English, Bernie Fuchs, Fred Otnes, Bob Heindel, Robert Peak

Guest Speakers have included:
1976: Lorraine Allen, Art Director, *Redbook Magazine*; Dick Coyne, Editor & Publisher, *CA Magazine*; John deCesare, Executive Art Director, Geigy Pharmaceuticals; Dick Gangel, Art Director, *Sports Illustrated*; Harvey Kahn, Artist Representative, Harvey Kahn Associates; Art Paul, Art Director, *Playboy Magazine*; Walt Reed, Editor, *North Light*; Neil Shakery, Art Director, *Psychology Today*. 1977: Herb Bleiweiss, Art Director, *Good Housekeeping*; John deCesare, Executive Art Director, Geigy Pharmaceuticals; Harry O. Diamond, Art Director, Exxon Corporation; Dick Gangel, Art Director, *Sports Illustrated*; Harvey Kahn, Artist Representative, Harvey Kahn Associates; David Merrill, Art Director, *Time Magazine*; Susan E. Meyer, Editor, *American Artist*; Lou Silverstein, Asst. Managing Editor, Corp. A.D., *The N.Y. Times*; Atha Tehon, Art Director, The Dial Press. 1978: Roger Black, Art Director, *Rolling Stone*; Bill Erlacher, Artist Representative, Artists Associates; Dick Gangel, Art Director, *Sports Illustrated*; Gerald McConnell, President, Graphic Artists Guild; Barbara Nessim, Artist; Jack O'Grady, President, Jack O'Grady Galleries; Al Parker, Illustrator; George L. Parker, V.P. Creative Services, Hallmark Cards, Inc.; Margery Peters, Art Director, *Esquire Magazine*; Maurice Sendak, Author & Illustrator. 1979; Sam Antupit, Art Director, Book of the Month Club; Walter Bernard, Art Director, *Time Magazine*; Darwin Bahm, Artists Representative; John deCesare, Consultant and Graphic Designer; Leo and Diane Dillon, Illustrators of Children's Books; Judith Jampel, Dimensional Illustrator; Herb Lubalin, Graphic Designer; Jerry McConnell, Graphic Artists' Guild; Lou Myers, Cartoonist and Writer; Howard Paine, Sr. Editor-Art, *National Geographic Magazine*; Jerry Pinkney, Artist; Leslie Segal, President, Corporate Annual Reports, Inc. Sacramento: Walter Bernard, Art Director, *Time Magazine*; Martin Pedersen, Graphic Designer and Publisher, *Nautical Quarterly*.

1976-79	1979	1980
On the banks of the Hudson River	**On the banks of the Sacramento River**	**On the banks of the Seine River**
The annual Seminar/Workshop programs were presented.	The first two-day Seminar/Workshop was presented in conjunction with the Sacramento Art Directors and Artists Club.	A special program, presented in Paris, France.

1981
On the banks of...

Write for information on this exciting Seminar/Workshop series. Bank on it!
John deCesare, Managing Director, The Illustrators Workshop, Inc., P.O. Box 3447, Noroton, Conn. 06820